The Entrepreneurs Platform LTD
71-75, Shelton Street,
Covent Garden,
London,
WC2H 9JQ
www.entrepreneurs-platform.com

Ordering Information:
Quantity sales. Special discounts are available on quantity purchases by corporations, associations, and others. For details, contact the publisher at the address above.
Orders by UK bookstores and wholesalers. Please contact Benjamin G. J. Barker by direct email BJGB@BenjaminGJBarker.co.uk or visit www.entrepreneurs-platform.com
Printed in the United Kingdom

Disclaimer

Although the author and publisher have made every effort to ensure that the information in this book was correct including third party percentages and prices at press time, the author and publisher do not assume and hereby disclaim any liability to any party for any loss, damage, or disruption caused by errors or omissions, whether such errors or omissions result from negligence, accident, or any other cause.

CONTENTS

CHAPTER

1

MY JOURNEY TO YOUR START UP
– THE BOOK

"No man ever steps in the same river twice, for it's not the same river and he's not the same man"
Heraclitus.

'A Switch in The Right Direction' has been written from my own perspective and viewpoint, to tell you of my journey into business and the small battles I have faced to date. For you, it may or may not be the right or wrong way, but my methods have most certainly earned me a living and enabled me to be self sufficient and never work a 9-5 job.

I do not claim to have "made it" as what defines "made it"? A Bentley in the garage of a seven figure home? What's your perspective on making it? We all have our own perspective; the Bentley and 7 figure home will be standard procedure in 10 years if inflation has anything to do with it. My sole intention of this book is to pass on any information I have learnt to help someone who has no knowledge, and to learn myself through the process.

My goal is to help the reader by showing them me as a person, who started just like they have with little or no knowledge or investment. This will help reduce the learning time for the reader through reading the tips and strategies I have placed within the book, which will help when pursuing a new business.

This book is written based on a few businesses I have

been gratefully involved in; if you wish to start a company similar to mine from reading this book, then great. But if you can gain some information from my case studies and life in business which enables you to start any business, this would be very satisfying for me.

This book contains methods, ideas and short cuts to a career within the cleaning, appliance and online sales industry and any small business; beginning your journey to self employment and becoming within the small percentage of freedom fighters within the country. I also include strategies to help you accomplish the right mindset, how to train your entrepreneurial mind, how to create an online presence and how to market and advertise any business.

Working for yourself has enormous benefits. One of those is the choice and freedom it can provide if implemented and managed correctly. I hope you enjoy the book and it encourages you to take the leap of faith into growing your own small business which one day will grow all by itself.

CHAPTER

2

INTRODUCTION

"We should not judge people by their peak of excellence; but by the distance they have traveled from the point where they started." Henry Ward Beecher

It's really true - now has never been a better time to set up your own business and become a true entrepreneur. What does the dictionary and myself define as a true entrepreneur? The dictionary calls an entrepreneur someone who sets up a business or businesses, taking on a financial risk in the hope for profit.

I feel an entrepreneur is an innovator, a designer, a creator, a chameleon morphing into different talents, characteristics and people.

Why is now the best time in history to start your own business?

According to *internetlivestats.com,* internet is being used by 40% of the worlds population compared to less than 1% in 1995. With even third world countries now gaining access to internet and mobile phones. Rural India now has more internet resources and technology today than what Russia had when they sent the man to the moon in 1961.

Technology is growing at such a fast rate, there is more people cutting free from the 9-5 job and starting their own business than any other time in history because of everyday improvements within the resources around us. Not to forget we see success wherever we go. Social networking platforms, TV, Radio, you hear of successful people everywhere. Naturally the human mind society has created wants to compare to other's and people are hungrier than ever.

Since the recession, the survival instincts within us kicked in, what was initially an idea to get by when times were tough, has developed into a realization of self worth and a boost in confidence. People are understanding they can also achieve the freedom which working for themselves can bring by using the resources and connections around them as oppose to the 1970's-80's when you had to climb the corporate ladder. The internet, phones, and technology were non existent, now we find ourselves abundant in ways to connect and control our life.

Just a few examples show we now have better designed resources enabling stronger feedback statistics for market research, finely tuned marketing strategies, advertising campaigns available to you; networking groups enabling you to connect easier and not forgetting easier ways to generate investment for new ideas. If we take a look at some of the wealthiest people on the planet who began multi billion pound businesses with less than £10,000 initial investment, when funds were not as easily accessible as they are today, such as Alan sugar, Richard Branson, there really is nothing holding you back.

A new generation is booming. It is far from how things once were, word of mouth was once the the only source of advertising, letters were the main method of long distance communication, phones and the internet were not available, and even within the era of limited technology - Coca Cola was founded 1892 it's now worth an estimated 56 billion.

Now is the greatest time in history to voice your talents, with platforms such as Facebook, Twitter, Instagram and LinkedIn. I stand by knowledge is power, but only once implemented, you could be a walking library but if it's not being put to use, or spread for your benefit, it is useless. This is why I believe word of mouth is still the main source of repeat business in regards to raising awareness for you and your product, once you and your product are known, this provides you with the credentials and foundations to build from.

This works in combination to who you know, as well as what you know; and although others would agree, I feel less of these people have mastered the strategy of using word of mouth and connecting with others to its full potential. Connections are important and we are very fortunate to be surrounded by the means to connect with others.

What do I feel is going wrong?

We are living in a very busy world where some businesses now tend to shoot for more likes on Facebook or up playing their product for sales than engaging with their customers. If you can buy your friends, followers and likes, is it really worth it long term? Is this really a solid connection? Todays technology has begun a new generation, but are we missing the crucial element of customer care and word of mouth which Coca Cola maintained when they began in 1982.

Should we focus more on engaging with our customers, listening to their opinions, taking time out to be present within the life of the supporters of our brand. The internet resources around us add great benefit to businesses, but with computers making non emotional decisions on a group basis is this contributing to the lack of customer care given.

We need to build with our customers and equip them with reasons to discuss our brand, empower our customers with the ability to have different ways to share our brand, letting them know they are important and their opinions matter.

According to a 2013 "Customer rage" study researched by an Arizona state university, 50% of American households have had a bad experience with a business in the last 12 months. What's worse is that the figure is up 45% since 2011 and has increased 32% since 1976! 56% of the people who were questioned, had nothing to compensate them for their bad experience with the business.

Is this good customer service? Am I right to discuss the lack of customer service within this book and methods on better strategies to address these concerns? I think so.

A fine example of a huge company who have their customers at heart is the bath bomb company 'Lush' who pull out all the stops where customers are concerned. 'Lush' were ranked number 1 by a poll created by 'Which?' in the UK for the best customer service in 2015. Why did they receive an 89% vote from customers? Simple. Customers love entering a shop with happy, helpful and greeting staff. Customers are impressed from the aromas upon visiting a 'Lush' store. Staff approach you, invite you to watch the bath bombs being created online. 'Lush' understand the RIO when prioritizing their customers, as this builds relationships which creates return sales.

Connecting with your customers on any business venture is a huge priority. Whenever I am present with an existing client or potential new client, I am present to them in that moment. I connect with them on a personal level and take time out to build a relationship with them; as oppose to doing the job and leaving. If you can master this and find a common ground of interest in conversation, your business and brand will explode.

Aim to replace the word sell with help, help your customers with your service. No one likes a needy salesman.

I believe everyone has a time in their life where they wish to work for themselves, had a great business idea, or thought of a creation to help others. I also believe that everyone *could* work for themselves and become an entrepreneur. How many people do you hear say at one time or another, I thought of this great idea the other day to put this with that, to create this. Well to me that is a product right there! Regardless if it will work or not.

But little fulfil this desire and majority remain within their comfort zone and familiarities of what they are use to because of the security it offers. Whilst some one who isn't necessarily smarter has executed their idea and is now on the way to the bank or may even be wiser than the person who did not try simply by becoming more of a risk taker. Believe me when I say, taking a risk whether you will fail or not, will put you miles ahead of any person who chooses not to take the risk. So execution really is what separates the talkers and the doers.

'But there's so many people now doing stuff, where do I fit in?'

True, there is more competition, more available resources for others. A job application which once had 5 applicants now has 50! Starting a business requires separation from the cliché gimmicks, you have to be unique, if you can be unique and separate yourself, this is your opening to fit in.

The only way to do this? Be honest and real. Reach your customers on a very normal level. I have made purchases with businesses in the past even when their product was not the best, delivery time not the fastest, but something they did have which made me forget about everything else was customer service and transparency.

I'm not talking about a call center phoning you for feedback. I mean real, true, friendly customer service and honesty. Doing more than you are paid to do, going the extra mile, as mentioned before you should be going out of your way to build a customer friendship with your clients. I believe hiring a company to take care of your internet campaigns, design your flyers, business cards can be done by most and is standard practice, hiring a professional to do a professional job is easy; but mastering word of mouth and building relationships with your clients is less likely by most. So maybe it is time to strip back the gimmicks, the poor sales tactics and go right back to how things once were.

Since word of mouth is the cheapest but most powerful source of advertising, it makes complete sense to master this and read more books concurrent with your future goals, become more social and not only grow and improve your business, but yourself in the process too.

'Ideas are easy; implementation is hard'

Although now could not be a better time to start a business; the more businesses started, the more which unfortunately fail. But is it unfortunately? Is failure what shapes us, builds our mental toughness and allows us to learn faster? I believe so. Personally I feel if success was a straight diagonally line upwards, everyone would be on the journey to financial freedom, yet according to HMRC figures only 5% of the country is on a pay wage over £60,000 a year. Bill gates after Harvard built a business called *'Traf-O-Data'* which did not gain momentum and subsequently failed. Was this what generated the idea for Microsoft?

Henry Ford, who developed and manufactured Ford cars failed with his previous 2 companies making him broke prior to becoming within the three most famous and richest men in the world.

Mark Cuban, prior to selling his company to Yahoo and becoming a multi-millionaire openly admits he was a failure at many things. He attempted to be a cook, a carpenter, a waiter. His words were *'I've learned that it doesn't matter how many times you failed. You only have to be right once. I tried to sell powdered milk. I was an idiot lots of times, and I learned from them all'*. The moral of the story is; fail as much and as quick as possible, never to be scared of failure, since failing actually positions you closer to success than one who never tried.

> **'Most great people have attained their greatest success just one step beyond their greatest failures' – Napoleon Hill**

Looking back in my time so far within business, and even personal relationships and life encounters - every single time I failed, something broke down, a relationship or friendship, it allowed further growth for me to move higher. If I had not experienced those failures, those down and low times, I can hand on heart pledge I would not have the perspective and understanding I hold today.

But how at a young age have I developed this understanding so quickly? An understanding it may take some years to figure out? Simple – It's because of how I position myself. I put myself in very uncomfortable situations all the time, this speeds up my learning process. When I fall back down, I jump straight back up, no delay, and I continue on. The only difference between me and another who may be asking themselves if they should visit the entrepreneurial road, is I don't think about why I fell down, I just get back up and keep going.

If I had a big knock back and spent a year back in my comfort zone, mentally bruised and anxious to leave my comfort zone once more, the guy who has already decided his going back out of his comfort zone again to have another go, has accomplished way more in that year than I have whilst trying to make my mind up. This is the difference, whilst your pottering along, someone is getting smarter, more experienced and positioning themselves for success regardless of age.

How can you possibly grow if everything is going right, if everyday is the same?

This book I am writing today, has been written after a failure and time in my life where I felt utterly hopeless. I began reading books on books, on other books, when one day I stumbled across something which read. "Stop reading books, and write one". So here I am.

Maybe if I hadn't of experienced the failures I have, the times in my life where I have felt so vulnerable, maybe I would have not began reading books, which means I wouldn't have read the book suggesting to write a book, and this book could have taken a further 20 years to materialize. But I thank my failures, the struggles and times where I felt hopeless, because this has been channeled into this book which I hope helps you.

Another example of a recent failure I had was loosing a great deal of money on the financial markets. Which is exactly what made me change the direction of this book to incorporate much more than it originally was planned to contain, this too is what created 'The Entrepreneurs Platform'. In June 2015 I began trading currency on the foreign exchange markets, to cut a long story short; China devalued their currency in August and amongst other factors, the stock markets crashed. I unfortunately had trades open and through naivety continued to keep my trades open which resulted in a margin closeout and loosing £17,000 in one morning.

Was I upset and angry? Was I about to throw myself of a bridge? No, I was not. Why? Because I had experienced failure in the past before, this built and prepared my mental toughness for further failures and losses in the future. I may have felt this way if I had not felt full failure and loss before.

In the last two weeks prior to losing the money, I began accepting it was a real possibility to lose it all. I used those two weeks of utter stress and worry to reflect on my current situation. I came to the conclusion that I was neglecting my gift by only concentrating on building my net worth and bank balance when really what I wanted to do was help people with the knowledge I had.

I was thinking about money, not adding value. So I forgot about the money I was about to lose, and instead focused my intentions on how to help others with what I already had. I believe as long as your intentions are in line with your end goal and you are consistently giving 110% in all areas of your life, the law of averages will reward you. So now when I have times where the future is blurry, I have faith that through my consistent effort something will always come up. I've lived so far with the belief that something amazing is just about to happen, and amazing things happen this way.

"All feelings, good or bad, are temporary"

What was stopping me before this to begin 'The Entrepreneurs Platform' to help connect others, to write a book? Simple, lack of confidence and believing I did not have enough credentials to teach to others. People tend to put a mental perceived barrier between themselves and the highly successful or celebrities. They feel unless they have millions in the bank, unless they have a million followers on Instagram, unless they are known; they can't reach out and write a book, they can't teach others.

This is rubbish, because if you learnt how to build a website, yet it was your first one, would you help someone who had never built a website? Of course you would, even though you've only done one and you may not be an expert, you would help with the knowledge you have gained so far and maybe learn the rest together? Which is why I decided to change this book, and set up The Entrepreneurs Platform.

This book is not a self help book to help you improve your social and communication skills, but it will help with strategies to connect better with your customers. It will give you a step by step guide of things to consider when planning and creating a brand and business. This book is written in a story telling way not in a to do list approach. I talk to a lot of business owners and I personally learn more in regards to business by listening to their unique personal tips and their story, than I have in a business class.

I am not claiming to know everything there is to know about business and building relationships or life. But what I can say, is I make people feel safe, and when people are made to feel safe and comfortable, they become honest. When they become honest, I can really understand their needs and fulfill those needs.

Imagine this book as you have just met a wise stranger in a coffee shop, you've brought them a coffee and sat and listened to their story of business, how they began, where they are now, and where they are heading. For the price of a coffee, you have walked away with a great deal of helpful information. Since the aim of reading books is to read from the authors perspective to increase your knowledge and awareness, treat this book as a key to opening a new perspective on business start ups.

Even if you can gain one lesson or one tip from this book providing you with good return on investment with money and time you have spent, I will be over the moon. This book also serves well for reference for myself. The book represents my journey so far and acts as an inspiration to me when I go off track and become forgetful of where this all began. A once young 17year old taking on the world, allowing no obstacle to come between him and his goal, leaving the house with no intentions of returning unless with money. Something we should all consider within ourselves, we are unstoppable, amazing, talented people who can achieve anything we set our minds too.

CHAPTER

3

THE BEGINNING OF MY STORY
AND BUSINESS

"In the end, it's not the years in your life that count. It's the life in your years." Abraham Lincoln

I left school at 15, in fact, I was expelled from school at 15. Being expelled was probably the best thing that ever happened to me. *Being expelled from school is the best thing that has ever happened to you?* Yes, because fortunately for me when I was expelled, I was allowed to still sit my GCSE exams at the school and join a second school for the remainder of my school life which meant I could complete even more GCSE qualifications. Although ultimately my GCSE's did not personally mean anything in the end, it was also the experience which played a huge part in my future.

After my school life had finished, I walked away with a folder full of certificates. I was always academic, but never could sit within a class full of 30 learning about the continents in which Christopher Columbus made settlements within. Hey! I remembered it though?

I joined Brighton City & Hove college straight after school to study carpentry & joinery. I went down this path as I always had a passion for working with my hands, creating and building physically and mentally. My dad was a carpenter; I guess most sons follow in similar footsteps to their fathers.

I stayed at college for 18 months, completing the first year, but not the second. Throughout my second year in college, I had a part time job, I say a job, but it was very illegitimate cash work for a local company stacking shelves in a warehouse for £80 per week in exchange for 15 hours of my life.

In my second year of college, 8 months in, I quit. I met a girl and continued to work my job remaining consistent in what I was doing for a few months. The girl I was with fell pregnant and I guess that is when you could say the game changed from a young, relaxed, and care free life to becoming a responsible adult needing to step up to the mark. But looking back now, I guess this process only sped up what was already there, which is who I am today.

I often wonder what would have happened if I hadn't of got my partner pregnant at 17. We all wonder how things would have ended up if things had of happened later or earlier. I use to always feel having my son was the beginning of my entrepreneurial journey, but looking back now, it was only the confirmation of an entrepreneur, not the beginning.

I can remember when I was 6 years old, drawing pictures under my bed which I had converted into an 'Art Attack' studio I saw on the TV. I use to sell them within the neighborhood for 5p each. A one off? Maybe. When I was 7-8 years old I use to charge family members 50p for massages, another sign? When I was in the last few years of secondary school, I use to ask the older people within my circle to buy cigarettes for me so I could resell them. I'd buy 20 cigarettes for £5.00 back then, and sell each cigarette for 50p each making £5 profit. I would make £10-15 profit a day, everyday. I use to walk up to the nearest shop from my village which was 45 minutes away and spend £5 on sweets and sell the following day at a profit. So I guess you could say I've always been entrepreneurial, I just didn't realize until I was forced to innovate when I had my son.

I can remember when I found out about my partner falling pregnant and ringing up the place where I currently worked to immediately quit. There was no way I could support a family on £80 per week and it was time to find something else. I booked in for my CSCS card enabling me to work in construction, I became self employed at 17 and got myself straight out onto the building sites. Oh what fun! Come snow, rain and shine I was there. Just waiting for those bricklayers to drop the next Mars bar wrapper off the scaffold for me to litter pick. Time could not have gone any slower. If you can relate to a job you have hated or even currently hate, you will understand like me the true meaning of clock watching. What felt like an hour, was really only 5 minutes.

But what choice did I have? I was a victim of todays society, a victim of the rat race. I had to be out there, bringing in the money for a soon to be family unit.

I continued to be a construction worker on and off for 8 months. The 4 months which followed on from this, I managed to work with a few local firms, cash in hand as a carpenter's mate, but working in small teams. This again did not work out, I was still in the same position as before, never quite feeling like I was working at my full potential.

By this time, my son had been born. We were not initially receiving any government aid in regards to social benefits and had a flat we were renting to pay for. Since my partner was working her part looking after our son with lack of sleep, it was only myself with the responsibility to create money. I can remember being so tight for money, spending £1 on a meal from the supermarket Iceland's to feed 3 of us per night; every night. This was not a one off - times were hard.

I was sat up every night with a notepad and pen writing

ideas, inventions, anything to think of an idea to bring more money home. This brainstorming plus frustration went on for months.

Then one day, something happened. A situation where most wouldn't blink an eye lid, a situation where most would think was normal, I saw an opportunity. I brought a second hand cooker from a guy running I guess a small business selling appliances. He delivered it to our flat. From what most people just be happy to receive a new cooker - my thoughts ran deeper than that. I have just paid this guy £160 for a used electric cooker. So how much did he get it for then?

Anyone who knows me will say my mind is always racing, thinking of new ideas, waiting for the big break. This time was no different, and since he left after delivering the cooker my mind was racing.

I have always been spontaneous. My jumping the gun in every situation has got be in a lot of trouble, but it has also made me a lot of money too. Probably the greatest thing about being spontaneous and a risk taker, is you learn twice as fast as the person who is the opposite. With being a professional risk taker, someone who creates a positive excuse as to why your doing what your doing as oppose to looking for negatives, you learn quicker because you fail quicker.

You trust the guy selling you the dodgy trainers as real ones, then learn to always buy real, you listen to the apparent business man giving you advice to do something a certain way, which ruins your idea, so you learn to choose others opinions more wisely, you take those risks and a lot of the time, it goes wrong. But that is the great part, because you eventually build a wealth of knowledge which allows you to see disaster from 2 miles away and help point others in the right direction.

The following day I took a risk. Understandably I had

little cash since purchasing a new cooker after the previous one would only cook half a pizza, resulting in 3 bouts of food poisoning! I had £20 in a bank account, that really was all until some wages I was waiting on for a laboring job I had completed the week before. I spoke to my partner who was anxious and told her I had decided to buy a used fridge. Bizarre? Yes, most would think so, especially as we had a fridge. She asked why, my plan was to sell it; at a profit of course.

So I got my hands on a used fridge. Took an inexperienced picture, and flogged it the same day for £40. "We'll have some of that" I can remember saying. £20 profit was a big deal when dinners were £1 each! Most would have thought of it as a fluke, and spent the money.

I risked the £40 and brought two more. Guess what? Sold those also the following day for £80. Looking back now I laugh, because I really did risk it all. Even once I was climbing up, I continued to risk, never afraid to start again. I began with nothing, so I could never lose it all.

Something Elon Musk said after he sold PayPal, the owner of Tesla, which always stays in my mind.

'My proceeds from PayPal were $180m. I put $100m in SpaceX, $70m into Tesla & $10m in Solar City. I had to borrow money for rent".

Elon Musk is a prime example of an extraordinary entrepreneur who has risked and continues to risk all he has for a vision

I began searching all the local directories. Gumtree, Friday-ad, Freecycle and eBay. I had to have a kitty, money for investing, money for spending. Ideally you want 3 sources, investing, spending and saving. But I wasn't at the saving stage just yet.

Those directories are full of electrical appliances. To start with, when ringing up to ask to see the item if possible try and see it plumbed in so you have an opportunity to see it working. Freecycle and any free site is full of free cookers, washing machines, dishwashers and more. I've even picked up free sofas, dining tables and chairs and sold at a huge profit.

I began picking everything and anything up. Mainly free to start with, but some purchased items too from eBay. My bathroom in my flat was massive, and it soon turned into an appliance store!

I had so much stock, I was turning over so much money, I soon took another risk. I began renting a single garage and storing and selling from there. This all happened within 3 months. I was on the road every single day doing deliveries and pick ups. I suggest to go buy yourself a used cooker for £30 and list it for £120 and watch what happens. Just honestly as a bit of fun and an experiment and taster of entrepreneurship.

So I spent 18 months at the garage buying and selling. I built up a huge reputation within my county. People would ring and ask if I was the cooker man, and I was. Until one day I was chased out of the garage by the local council for making cash sales from a residential garage! So I moved to a bigger place.

Why would people want to buy and what was the secret? The exact secret as to how my business grew from £20 to creating over £2,000 a month in profit within the first 6 months to over £50,000 yearly in profit; is because I travelled sometimes 100 miles to get my appliances. In my first 6 months I managed to find enough stock within my local area to consistently supply demand. But the supply began to grow and grow and I began searching further and further to feed the demand. Some people would call me crazy for travelling 100 miles to buy a dirty cooker for £30. But it wasn't crazy when I sold it the following day at £180, for a £150 profit.

Customers would never travel 100 miles to collect a cooker, let alone 25 miles. They want to ring up, buy the cooker, and have it delivered the same day if not the next. They want convenience, just like McDonald's and other fast food restaurants, its convenience. Just like a mechanic; yes, you may know how to change your own brake pads, but you would prefer just to take it to the mechanic and have it done today. Everything is convenience nowadays, just like my cleaning company which I will discuss later. Anyone can clean, anyone can hire a carpet cleaning machine, but people do not choose to do it them selves when there is a service which provides this.

This is the main reason my business and most others thrive, especially when times were much harder 4 years ago from the recession. The second reason it thrived was because of variety. It was always important for me to appeal to more than just one audience, I achieved this by selling everything.

If cookers were slow, fridge freezers overtook. I would say the third reason it thrived was because of money management. I religiously never spent the money I originally paid. If I paid £30 for an appliance and sold for £180 I would always keep minimum £30. 99% of the time I would keep double of the price paid, to always reinvest. To begin with I was happy to wait so I would reinvest the full £180 and purchase 6 more then take my cut when it was ripe.

You need to completely separate yourself from the business. When I paid for fuel, I did not pay for it, the business did. When I paid for stock, the business paid for stock. The business paid me.

I advertised on the same sites I brought from. I had two phones, one for buying, one for selling so numbers did not repeat on the ads. On one occasion I had some one ring up stroppy that I had re-advertised the cooker I had just purchased from them for £40 for a hefty £200 the same day. So understandably people do not want you buying their appliance to sell at a profit. On collection I would explain it was for a new property I was moving into. If I had more than one in the back of my car they noticed, I would say I collected them for property rentals for a friend.

I advertised in more than one location, I am based in Sussex, therefor East and West Sussex were covered, different delivery charges. Collection was preferred but delivering 3 or more in one location was preferred even more. Three lots of delivery charges for three deliveries to one location, costing me only one delivery in fuel.

Fast forward a year, my personal cooker at home broke. I've never been one for convenience, especially not back then. I guess you could say that is how I learnt so much. Everything was done by me, and if I did not know how to do it. I would learn how to.

Our cooker was broken as it was blowing out cold air. Yes, I sold them - but I had no idea on how to repair them. I researched and learnt about elements, how to change them and purchased one off eBay. Unbelievably surprised at how easy it was to fit, I began offering this service in addition to sales. *Element repairs £99.* Can you believe how many elements need to be replaced in Sussex?

Now doing sales and repairs. I began to offer installation. Wiring an electric cooker into a property is very simple. Majority of customers just do not know about this, why would they need too? Convenience has to be one of the biggest reasons most businesses thrive - this was no different.

I began charging a set fee for installation and a set fee for taking away the old appliance. In total I would buy a used cooker for £30, sell for £180 with £30 installation with normally £20 delivery as most were local and £10 to take away the old appliance. £240 in total. A high percentage of the cookers or appliances I use to take away were still very much fit for resale. Some needed elements, new control knobs etc. I would order these small parts and resell that cooker also for £150-180. On some occasions I would make a sale including installation and delivery, taking away the old one, and sell their old one the same day. £400 profit from £30.

What do I think you need?

You need to start with a van. I started with a hatchback can you believe it! Then an estate, then a van. Vans pay for themselves. If I had 4 to pick up, that was two trips in a hatchback, double the fuel; whereas a van was only one trip.

You need to mimic your style on your ads with the layout and what you write. This creates a reputation and style, subconsciously people remember this and people begin to recognize you. I purchased a gold number from a website, It's a unique number such as 07999 123455. Much better than a normal one and it stands out.

You need a premises to store the items you are selling, whether its sofas, appliances, or anything you can get your hands on.

Further down the line I had a WordPress website designed. I chose WordPress because I personally could log into it and upload recent stock. I had so many ads on advertising sites such as Google it was hard for a customer to know what was still available, a website therefor allows them to see what is and is not and additionally benefits your brand. I speak on the prices of WordPress sites further along in the book. Alternatively, you could learn how to build a WordPress site yourself, which is very easy.

I am now in a much larger premises, I have branding, logos; a business name. The set up is more professional, I deal with suppliers now for used stock as opposed to the publics items. Although I would never let a good deal go.

Other than sales, you could put yourself on an engineering course for less than £1500 to learn everything about fixing all appliances to additionally offer this too. There are a few locations within the UK who operate these courses, potential full time stream of income there amongst sales and installations. More than one van on the road and so on.

The niche has been extremely rewarding for me, if you cannot think of an idea as of yet, begin this one. You really do not need much investment to begin with, I began with £20 and patiently built it from scratch. Listen and put to work what I have said, I promise it will work. Appliances are an item which people rely on and they will forever be in consistent demand.

*I would really suggest if you want to know where to start with entrepreneurship is to look up some used appliances, or maybe a free sofa, buy and collect and have a go at selling to give you the opportunity to learn the techniques required to close a sale, and build your social skills.

CHAPTER

4

My Business and What Happened Next?

"What you do today can improve all of your tomorrows." Ralph Marston

I continued the appliance business; it still remains today. That story began in 2012, writing this book now towards the end of 2015 much has happened. I have always been one to not become I guess bored as such, but always needing to be challenged. I set up new ideas, but once the challenge had finished or required less of my input, I find myself searching for the next exciting opportunity.

In 2013 I wanted a change. I never wanted to finish the appliance company, but I wanted to supplement my current income. One day I came across a link inviting me onto a website which was the middle man between wholesale suppliers and customers. It boasted that a membership subscription enabled you to see a full database of the UK's biggest wholesalers of discounted stock. To good to be true surely? So as opposed to paying for the full membership, there was an option to buy the individual suppliers details to view what it was about. I chose this, and it really was true. After paying it unlocked the suppliers hidden website and all of their details and stock.

I include the sites details in my blueprint on www.entrepreneurs-platform.com

I signed up for the full membership and could not believe the amount of UK suppliers available. I spent the entire night looking through hundreds. For any like minded entrepreneur out there reading this, you know what the feeling is like when you think you have hit the next big goldmine!

I got to work - brainstorming. I searched eBay for some of the items I had found from these suppliers, the items were selling. Some eBay sellers were selling thousands, hundreds and thousands of even just one item I had found. To say I was excited was an understatement. Out of all of the suppliers I really saw great potential in around 10. I researched 20-30 products from each, strong solid and reliable products with a track record of selling on platforms such as eBay. Easy to pack, light and a good mark up. I got my mark up prices from other sellers on eBay and undercut everyone by £0.10-0.50

After choosing 80 product lines to sell from the 300 products I had researched; I began writing up eBay descriptions for each individual item. This took some time and as I did not have the product in physical form yet so I had to use my selling tactics. I now had 80 product ideas, 80 descriptions ready to copy and paste into eBay and 80 strong researched prices which I would sell my products for.

The business took me 2 months to set up before even buying stock, everything had to be researched. The markets, products, you need to budget and allow for final VAT on items you purchase, minimum orders to take into consideration from suppliers, delivery time from suppliers. Descriptions and returns policy's had to be written. PayPal accounts set up and eBay account transfers. If one product sold out from the 80 you had listed, you could not rebuy that one product until others had sold out because of minimum orders, so it was finding a fine balance between how many to order originally. There is a lot to take into account.

Of course, I needed an eBay account. But not just any eBay account. I needed an eBay account which had no selling restrictions, one which had a standing reputation, one which was a top rated seller, power seller etc. How could I win my customers over and have them choose me over my competition if my eBay account was smalltime. So I did a quick search on eBay and believe it or not there are a few sellers who sell their eBay account!

So I brought an eBay account with a few thousand feedbacks, no selling restrictions, a power seller and top rated seller etc. for £800.00

I invested £3,000 into stock spread over my suppliers and purchased 80 strong lines. I took good original photos, copy and pasted my premade descriptions in when listing and on my first day of trading made £50 profit. Result!

The business went from strength to strength. The beauty of it was although initially it took a huge chunk of my time and life away before I could fine tune everything for it to take much less of my time to run, I did not need the money it made. The appliance money paid me everything I needed, so I used all money made from the eBay business and re-invested it.

My first month I made £500 profit from 3-4 hours per day running. Second month was £800 because I reinvested and added 20 new product lines from the 300 researched. Third month I made £1200, because I used the previous month's money to reinvest. By the time I sold the business for just under £20,000 the business required one hour per morning to run and was bringing in consistently £1800 a month or more in profit.

Why did I sell it? Of course, I needed a new challenge. I

still have the blueprint available for this business, I sell the blueprint and it includes the full set up in beginning this business; the suppliers, products researched, descriptions, photos, prices to list for. All you need is an eBay and PayPal account. You do not need to limit your selling on just eBay, or even eBay at all. I was an Amazon seller too and also had a Facebook selling page where I sold 5-10% of the stock.

Get yourself a creative name and create a brand and logo. Do not include your personal name, use something unique. Register for a franking postal machine which most of the time are free, you are just charged a premium on the franked stamp. Purchase and follow the blueprint, it is a very convenient and worthy business to have.

After the business sale went through of my eBay business, I was left twiddling my thumbs, looking for the next adventure. If you had asked me then would I be running a cleaning business a year later I would have laughed; but that's what happened. I will now walk you through my next business.

CHAPTER

5

WHAT FOLLOWED?

"Failure will never overtake me if my determination to succeed is strong enough." Og Mandino

My cleaning company was created through a phase in my life of depression. I was in a depressive state for months to say the least. This never stopped me from doing what I love and live to do, which is entrepreneurship. There is nothing more rewarding to me than building something from the ground up, and witnessing it grow. It is quite extraordinary to create something which regularly provides you an income and pushes you forward to becoming self reliant on yourself; It's a real confidence booster. This business partly helped remove me from where I was mentally at that point in my life.

The cleaning industry is a great niche to be involved in. According to the Office of National Statistics 2012, The UK's contract cleaning market was valued at 4.7 billion in 2011, considering majority of cleaners are private individuals working on a regular client basis, there is a huge potential for even more specialized cleaning companies to form.

I aim to provide you with as much information I can on the subject, since I do run a cleaning business myself. The aim of this book as mentioned at the start, is to give you an insight into the cleaning industry in simple terms among my other businesses. Advice you on how to get started, where to actually begin based on my story and mistakes and how to talk the jargon. It's aimed to cut your learning curve in half, save you time and be more productive. It's also a good book to refer to for all small business start ups.

When I first began carpet cleaning which led onto all round cleaning, I had no knowledge what so ever. In fact, I didn't initially even want to become a carpet cleaner. One sunny Sunday afternoon, I was sat in my mother's garden, thinking of new businesses to start shortly after selling the eBay business. I was scrolling through businesses for sale on eBay, and one came to my attention.

"A carpet cleaning package for sale"

It was on a low auction price and had little time left. The listing had my interest, so I clicked to find out more. I looked through the pictures and initially wrote down all the items brand and model numbers that the sale came with. I researched these items and realistically priced what I thought I could break down and sell these items at. With what the current auction price was on, I would make a good profit. So this was plan A, initially.

Plan B, was to actually be a carpet cleaner. But if you had asked me a month before; 'Ben, do you think you could become a carpet cleaner?'. With my lack of knowledge, I would have laughed and said no. I continued to watch the listing, it remained at the same price. I then set a price in my head of what I was prepared to pay.

It's really important you set a price, and always stick to it. Too many people let their impulses get the better of them and cloud their judgment when it's running down to the end of the auction. I've seen countless people at auctions go well above their initial price agreed in their head, simply because they become possessive and convince themselves it's theirs.

Always stay within budget.

The listing was down to the last hour with price remaining the same, I was the highest bidder and it had not yet reached my maximum bid I was prepared to pay. On the last ten minutes the price began increasing, until the price almost reached my maximum budget. I won the auction just below the price I set.

Overwhelmed, I did not know what next to do. I had to make a quick decision on whether I would break down the items and sell individually, or take the route of learning a new skill, a new business; and become a carpet cleaner. I chose the latter.

I began researching within my area the need for a carpet cleaner and looking to see who else was on the scene. Within my area, there was only 3 other carpet cleaners. I had a quick glance at their sites, their reviews, prices and wording and got to work. I could see there was a gap in the market for a professional carpet cleaner to fit in and scope to expand. I felt that within my area, the carpet cleaners available didn't have the professional touch I wanted to give, it looked more like a hobby to them from my perspective.

Seeing a gap, I then began thinking about funding. Thinking of ways to raise the money needed for this entire business purchase, I decided to ring my bank. I was in a good position with the bank as I already had a business account which had been opened 12 months prior. I had already been accepted for a personal loan before and paid it off well before the due date. So I was in a good position to borrow money to fund the business, but it wasn't guaranteed until I asked. I spoke to the bank, explained the situation, and asked for £7,000 to fund a new business start up. I had to go through questions upon questions, which lasted a painful 45 minutes on the phone. Luckily the checks went through and I was granted the money needed.

I decided not to invest any money or savings of my own into this venture. I understand the reader may not have had a previous or present business account, previous loans, or be in a recognizable position in the eyes of their bank to receive funding. I will touch on good credit builders and other ways to obtain funding and investment later in the book for a complete newbie to business start ups.

To recap-

Step 1. Thinking of a business idea
Step 2. Research the market and industry
Step 3. Funding and investment for your venture.

How do you research the market to see if your business idea is a valid needed service?

If your idea is a product, the best way is to ask. Ask the public what they think of your concept and whether they would purchase the product. Create a questionnaire and publish on social networking sites such as Facebook. Ask family and friends their opinions on your product. Although I personally wouldn't take the final word of friends or family as to whether to pursue it or not, but opinion on your product is a good start.

Research online your competitors. Are there many? How well are they doing? Where are they based? Maybe your competitors are in a different county or even country in which case this gives you a huge opportunity to enter the market.

Find out how much the industry your product matches is worth. Is it a big industry? Is your product needed?

Will your product require updating, add-ons to stay current? Or will the product die out after a year?

Speak to people within the industry you are entering, people who have achieved what you wish to achieve.

If your idea is a service, such as a carpet cleaning for example. Research the local area for competition. Checkatrade and local tradesman directories are a good start, find out how long these service providers have been established.

You also need to decide why you are entering the market with your service or product. What's your mission? Your purpose? Are you trying to improve your customers lives with your product or service? What differentiates you and your service in comparison to your competition?

Are you solving a direct problem? For example, is there a lack of carpet cleaners within your area? Or are the carpet cleaners which are established missing something you can offer?

Finally, do you think you can profit from the service or product you are providing? I understand as an entrepreneur the answer is a yes. We know it will work, without that passion we wouldn't pursue the idea, but lack of research prior to embarking on a new business venture is like driving from your house to a destination 300 miles away; without a satnav or a map. Unless you have done it before, its unlikely you will find your way.

Unless you have plenty of money left over, I wouldn't personally recommend using all of your savings for a new business venture when there are many alternatives to funding which help with tax purposes. Using your own finances to fund a business is called 'bootstrapping'. Bootstrapping your way through business understandably can be beneficial as it requires no involvement from other investors. The disadvantage is the potential hold on growth due to lack of financial support.

I have always kept personal money away from my business unless required and due to the risk factor. With the idea in place, the research looking promising and the funding secured; I messaged the seller and arranged a time to pick up. The package I had purchased included a van which was sign written already. The business had branding, a website; and looked ready to go with minimal effort from the design perspective and no need for the process of thinking of names and logos. A carpet cleaning machine was included with an agitator, a carpet cleaning wand, sets of hoses, a water tank, a jet wash sprayer, multiple chemicals to use when cleaning carpets, and also chemicals to clean and valet cars. Hence the jet wash and water tank. Meaning I also had the option to offer the cleaning of cars also.

I had no idea what any of this was, how it worked and no knowledge of how to clean carpets. Closest I had come to a carpet cleaning machine was one time when I hired a carpet cleaner to clean some carpets in a house I was moving out of. He turned up with a DIY rug doctor, I thought that was the best machine you could get and never questioned him. If I had known what I know now back when he cleaned my carpets, I would have asked him to leave when he turned up with a rug doctor. I'm not saying these machines aren't good, but there's a reason why you can hire a supermarket carpet cleaning rug doctor; or a professional carpet cleaner!

We agreed a time and place to meet, I collected the money needed then set off. Excited and nervous, I arrived an hour later. When I arrived, I began inspecting the equipment. Not really knowing what to look for I began looking for the obvious.

Rust, damaged parts, anything which looked like it had great wear and tear. All looked well, so I took the van for a test drive. Couple of knocks but I was too excited to care about minor knocks whilst driving or anything which didn't seem to severe. I wasn't a mechanic, but I had basic knowledge of cars and vans, having owned enough and had enough breakdown on me. Seemed all ok to me, some sign writing was hanging off but I though what the heck, I can get that patched up.

I went down the route to purchase this business as a package, I will soon explain how to set this business up from scratch, with no van, previous business name, graphics or equipment.

We discussed money; I asked for the login details to the current business website and any other associated business related logins and passwords I may need to transfer to me. He explained he had them, but not too hand.

This was my first mistake by leaving without these details and trusting the seller to provide them later on. In hindsight I wish I had got these before leaving, see the problem is; if I don't have the login details to transfer to me, I can't change the location of the business and google will still register my business in his location. Which means the website sign written on the van means nothing if I can't make it live by logging in.

So at this point, I had a good van with a few knocks, some sign writing which needed touching up in places, and a variety of machines, tools, and chemicals for the job. I set off home and went to see some local sign writing tradesman to explain that I'd like the sign writing patched up in certain places.

To my surprise, he advised me to strip the whole van of the current sign writing and start fresh, I asked why? He went on to say; sign writing has a life span and for all I know this could have been on here for a few years. The second reason was because the sign writing had been made specifically for this business by another sign writer, this template had been made by them, so the design would be difficult to copy and match.

I was taken back by this initially; I had not allowed for new sign writing within my budget. I didn't even know it had a specific life span, or anything about matching old sign writing, or anything in fact on this topic.

"Another lesson learnt, buying in excitement is fun, being spontaneous is great fun. But when purchasing a business package, ensure you always view before buying."

I now factored in that I needed to allow for new sign writing so I phoned a few more local trades-men. I was quoted £100 just to remove the old sign writing including all residue and machine polish the van ready for new graphics. I stand firm that most tasks can be completed yourself, if you are a new business start up it's vital you cut costs if you can by putting in the man power. I decided to have a go at removing the sign writing myself, watching videos on YouTube on the easiest and quickest way to do so, I got to work - another opportunity to learn something new!

I spent the whole day removing the writing and polishing the van with a polisher from a DIY store. The job was basically free; minus paying for the lunch of the people who gave me a helping hand!

Now I had the dilemma, do I stick with the same business name, same graphics and same text as before on the van? I still hadn't received login details for old website so I still couldn't change the location of the business and market the same business in my area. So this is when I decided to start completely from scratch. Now I'm going to show how to start from scratch.

In hindsight, I wish I had done this before. The reason being most business packages are fantastic; packed with previous reputation, great websites, all the basics in place to minimize business start up times. In which case it's just a matter of marketing it now in your area and training, similar to a franchise opportunity. Mine did not have the website any longer, I couldn't just change the location on google and just market it now in my area, the sign writing had gone, it was all just a blank canvass. I now had the job to think of logos, a name for the business, text, slogans, catchy phrases.

Initially I didn't allow for this, the time or finances to cover this. The story of business I guess! So I grabbed a pen and began jotting down ideas and logo designs. The original name was House Proud Valet, as they cleaned carpets and cars. So house proud for carpets, and valet for cars. I wanted to keep the house proud part, but change the valet. I decided I didn't want to clean cars, I wanted to focus on growing just one part of the business first, carpet cleaning.

They say the jack of all trades, is the master at none. I wanted to master carpet cleaning and learn all I could before adding other relevant services to it. It's silly to take on too much initially, especially more than one thing which isn't relevant, because then it involves mastering, marketing, and advertising two services.

I liked the sound of House Proud Finish, I wanted my customers to be house proud and it to be a finish we provided. Most importantly, this is one of the things I wanted to prioritize; a brand. I cannot stress enough how important a brand name is. There is a huge difference between Ben's carpet cleaning or House Proud Finish. The reasons being - Ben's carpet cleaning can't then offer oven cleaning, car cleaning, or patio cleaning as well; it limits you. The other main reason is people recognize brands, logos, they become household names.

Bens lawn mowers never became a household name, but 'lawnmowers r us' has a greater potential. Something simple and catchy works well. Once this is established, the services you can then offer are endless, you can create new departments or work van divisions who deal with different parts of the business. For example; a division on the road who take care of oven cleaning, a division who take care of end of tenancy cleans, one for carpet cleaning and so on. This is the potential, Ben's carpet cleaning limits that potential. I decided to stick with House Proud Finish, next I had to think of a logo.

Obviously a house sprung to mind, I wanted the logo to be relevant to the name, so a house made sense. I drew some vague ideas and went to see a local business specializing in logo design, t shirt print, and business cards. I explained the situation including the name and brand and said I'd like a logo designed. Within a week, one had been created. I came back to view and I was amazed. If you visit my website, it is a great logo. They then pieced House Proud Finish next to it and underneath read, 'professional carpet and upholstery'. I opted to go with a blue colour scheme, since blue represents cleaning and water. With a silver backing, almost like a silver lining.

The company done a fantastic job at designing and I booked in to have the van done and business cards designed with them also. Van sign writing cost me approximately £350.00, this will change depending on what you would like done.

I recommend to go for a mid range business card, a premium card option, nothing amazingly flashy. Depending obviously on what your design consists of some require a glossy finish, some a matt finish. But do not go for the cheap option, it's important you invest in the musts, vehicle sign writing, a good business card design on a good material is very important, all these things represent you as a business. These purchases act as an investment, not so much an expense.

Next step was thinking about a website. You have a few choices in regards to a website. HTML based websites are code, unless you have experience in writing and formatting code, these are not as easy to build or regularly update and change.

The second option is WordPress based websites. WordPress based websites are so easy to manage, change, and add to, even someone who isn't great with computers. WordPress is more of a type your text, then click update and publish. HTML is writing out your text, inputting lots of code surrounding it, updating and publishing. My passion isn't in HTML coding, I've tried to learn it before, but decided to go with the more convenient option based on what I needed which was a site I could personally and regularly update myself.

Website designing isn't cheap, it can range from a couple of hundred pounds to thousands. This isn't even including SEO, google ranking, and any relevant plugins you may require. So I designed how many pages I liked and spent hours and hours researching other carpet cleaner's websites. Remember also that I had not completed any training yet, I still did not know the process of even how to use a carpet machine, what chemicals I had to use, and what the process was. So I needed to learn from others, read what others had to say and put it all into my own words, imagining if it was me who was providing the service.

I needed to become in my head a carpet cleaner to create the text needed. So I formed 4 pages. Home, what's our process, frequently asked questions and a contact us page. I spent a few days filling these pages with great information from reading what others had put and already began learning the process and was one more step ahead.

I recommend not putting a price list page just yet, obviously research other local carpet cleaners and base your prices around theirs. Then maybe initially slightly go cheaper than theirs to start with, because if a customer won't choose you over an established business, they will choose you over price. So have a written down list of your prices, so you stay the same and you are consistent.

The reason why I wouldn't recommend putting a price list on your website just yet, at least until your established, is because it may throw the customer off straight away from viewing. Whereas If there is no price list and they really want to use you, they will call you to ask the price. The moment they've called for a price you have their attention already. If your sales pitch is good, by the time you have them, price will not matter anymore. That is the tip - keep it away from them at first until established.

Once ready, I began looking at designers who created WordPress sites. From previous experience of the appliance website I had, I looked on eBay for website design. eBay is an amazing place for great deals. You really can find someone who designs 5 pages, a years free hosting, free logo design if needed, a free domain name for example 'www.houseproudfinish.com' with completion in less than a week for less than £50.00.

Amazing really in comparison to other price quotes I received. If you are feeling really confident, you could purchase a WordPress hosting and domain package from a supplier such as GoDaddy.com, download a theme you like for free or opt for a premium paid theme from a supplier such as 'Theme Forest' and build your own site from scratch!

Once designed; you can then add more pages yourself, edit content and add pictures with ease. I purchased a great deal from a reputable seller on eBay with positive feedback on building websites. The whole deal cost me £39.00 and included all of the above with completion in less than 5 days. With the website now in place and live, the van due in for sign writing, business cards ordered, the next step was training.

I have always liked the idea of self teaching as mentioned earlier, I've always believed if they can do it, I can also. But sometimes it isn't always about that and investing in certain parts of a business is a must, you can't do everything alone. Most services such as logo design and professional van sign writing will need to be left to the expert in the field, training also falls under this category.

I first brought a piece of old carpet and I can remember laying it out in my back garden, setting up a machine I had never used - had no idea how to use, then just stood there trying to figure it out. I added the water and some chemical which I believed to be the detergent needed to clean with and connected all the hoses together. I laugh now, because I even connected the hose to the exhaust, I didn't even know it was an exhaust. It blew the water through the wand instead of vacuuming and sprayed water all over my garden. I eventually had it kind of set up and began passing the wand through this old piece of carpet. It looked no different.

So I packed up, with the machine full of water as I hadn't yet gained the knowledge on how to empty it. I started to question everything and didn't know whether my set up was enough to provide the standard I wanted to provide. So I looked into training, I initially underestimated this; which was a huge mistake. I looked around at courses and it made sense to go with the manufacturers of my machine I brought with the business, they offered courses, chemicals, sales, repairs, everything I could ever need. I think loyalty is important, if I was going to go with any one I wanted them to ideally be my long term contact. The manufacturer was Ashbys - anyone looking into carpet cleaning would have heard of them. I can't speak on other brands and manufacturers as I haven't used others.

But what I can say is Ashbys in Kent offer unbelievably great service with advice and equipment. They are a family run business and remain family orientated, which adds great value to their business when dealing with it's customers.

Other manufacturers and brands which supply equipment and offer great customer service, courses, training, and ongoing support are Prochem, Alltec, NCCA (national carpet cleaner's association). Length of courses and depth of training varies from one to another. I advise you to look into each and decide for yourself which best suits you. Location is a big factor, ideally you'd like something local to you especially if you'd like to use their ongoing repairs and support for the future.

Google is a great way to start, simply inputting 'carpet cleaning courses'. I booked Ashbys carpet cleaning course online, fortunately enough for me, it was only a few weeks from the date I booked. I booked one day for beginners.

Upon arriving, there was roughly 10 of us. The atmosphere was very relaxed, everyone present is there for the same reason, so already you all have something in common with each other. Derek Ashby went through all elements of the carpet cleaning process, demonstrating as he went. Lunch was included which was a great bonus! The building in which the training took place was their headquarters. This is a great benefit for new people to the industry as all the equipment and chemicals are on display to view. Ashbys also have a third party financing company used for customers to lease and finance their equipment. I will go more into financing and leasing later on.

After leaving the training day I had picked up a vast amount of knowledge which I eagerly wanted to put to use. With the van now sign written and business cards in place, the website built and training completed; I was almost on the way to having enough under my belt to begin my first cleaning job.

Next step was thinking about public liability insurance. A big factor for anyone is price - everyone wants the best price. The second determining factor is reputation of the company your deciding to go with, it's important to read reviews on your public liability insurer to see how they really deal with their claims process and to also find out any hidden extras and if they are true to their word. Another thing to consider is if they insure you for everything you need them to insure you for. For example; they may insure you for cleaning the carpets, but not for moving furniture to gain access to all of the carpet. They may not insure you to use certain equipment to get your finish, there's so many clauses used so make sure to read over everything.

Another factor to take into consideration is if you wish to expand your business in the future. Are you hoping to add on oven cleaning, end of tenancy cleaning, hard floor cleaning? If so, look for an insurer who can accommodate this in the future if you wish to expand. A great insurer available and one who I use myself is 'Gleaming insurance'. Simple set up with a great price and recognized within the cleaning industry. "Simply business" and "tradesman saver" are good - there are many options available to you from a simple search on google.

You will also need to think about how you will represent yourself when you arrive at your customer's house - what I mean by that is how you will dress. If you have had a good logo designed there's no reason why you can't have this printed onto a polo shirt or T-shirt. You will be surprised how many carpet cleaners arrive in their normal clothes; all these things contribute towards brand awareness. Visit the same place you had your van sign written and business cards made and get yourself a quote for some brand clothing to be made. I'd recommend the embroidery route first, initially more expensive in regards to the first set up fee, but it's a long term investment.

CHAPTER

6

MARKETING ADVERTISING AND SETTING UP WITH MY BUSINESSES

"Timid salesmen have skinny kids." Zig Ziglar

With the public liability and your branded clothing in place - the next step is marketing and advertising. You will need a reasonably big sized budget for this, long term. Although I will discuss further on in this book free ways to market your business.

Trouble is when you don't have any before and after pictures, how can you show your potential clients your work? The best way is to offer it for free - Yes I said free. When you first begin you will need to do a few jobs for free, or at least for next to nothing. This will allow you a few reviews, the foundation of word of mouth, your company awareness and most importantly before and after pictures.

You have your machine, you've been on your training, been advised on the best chemicals and the process, all you now need to do is offer your services initially for free. I can't stress enough how brand awareness over profit is important. I've completed jobs for free, thrown in so many freebies and when I first started offered deal after deal and cut prices numerous times. It's very important for the first 3 months you do not think about great amounts of money. The first 3 months need to be spent on awareness, awareness and awareness.

"Awareness is priceless. I'd choose people knowing my brand over profit any day, because profit comes with awareness"

Create a business Facebook page, if you already have a personal profile, you can add this page to your personal page by clicking create a page for a business. Once this is created; set your profile picture and cover photo to your new business logo.

Create an enticing description about your business clearly displaying what you do and who you are. Once this is designed type into your search bar on your personal profile for local selling groups. For example; I would type - 'Sussex selling page', 'Sussex buy and sell'. This will bring up loads of local groups to your location who sell items. Majority of these groups are laid back with their rules and allow businesses to post their services on their page.

Also type in your local area; so for me it would be 'Sussex', followed by 'business directory'. There are so many directories on Facebook specifically aimed at customers looking for local tradesman. The amount of groups available to join are endless. According to Huffington post; Facebook claim to have 24 million unique users every day. You are missing a massive business opportunity if you are not putting out on social networking who you are. I guarantee you will receive hundreds of queries from this source.

Now your Facebook page is designed and you have joined all the local Facebook groups, you need to post on all of these sites who you are. So for example –

"(Your company) are offering a new promotional offer of 5 free carpets cleaned within a 15km radius of (your area) for the first 5 people who comment, like and share this post. We are new to Facebook and hope to gain

new followers and interest of our business. We offer professional carpet and upholstery cleaning within (your area). The best prices guaranteed (include your website URL here and your business Facebook page URL)."

This will generate interest and guarantee your first 5 bookings.

See the thing is people may not even want their carpets cleaned, but the fact your offering it for free, what have they got to loose? Physiologically everyone knows people love free stuff! Once you are there doing the job, they get to know you and see your work, it is inevitable they will then recommend you if you've repeated what you've learnt in your training.

Word of mouth as mentioned earlier is the strongest in my opinion form of awareness. In the past there's been hundreds of times I have cleaned the carpet of a client, maybe even just a £30 job; but through that I've then cleaned their sisters, mums, uncles and grand-parent's carpets - amounting to hundreds of revenue in work, priceless awareness and free advertising. Ensure to take good before and after pictures and loads of them. Now you've had your first 5 clients, you have your before and after pictures, you can create a 5th page on your website for a gallery and upload the media to this. You can also kindly ask your 5 customers if they would leave you a review on your business Facebook page, or a testimonial on your website, a possible 6th page for your website!

Now your started, 5 people know who you are. That's 5 more people who knew before and 5 people who if they decide they need carpets cleaned again, or their families and friend's carpets; who are they going to call? YOU!

You've now got your reviews and pictures. Keep up

with the Facebook advertising by always throwing it in people's faces consistently of what you offer and who you are. Maybe switch it up, so one week with your post on the selling sites and directories, add a different before and after picture. It's really important you come across professional, I understand right now your new, but the act as if mentality goes a long way initially.

"If you're not where you want to be right now, act like you are there already, and you will become it"

You need to act as though you are a sought after company, people need you, your so busy! Get your bookings in quick people! But word it without sounding too desperate. This idea of advertising will need to be regularly taken care off and always checked, you cannot afford to miss messages and comments from potential new clients. If you leave communicating and responding too long they may ask for a quote from the competition!

What other forms of advertising could you use?

Go to yell.com and create yourself a free listing with them. Follow the details, they do also offer a paid service which gets you within the top results, this is your call. Type into google "(Your location) business directories", also visit online tradesman databases, anything related to directories which you can register your business with - this is all awareness and positioning you and your business. When people type in your name into google you don't want just your website to pop up. You want a yellow page's advert, directory adverts, you want to fill that first google page and be everywhere.

Go to gumtree.com and create a business advert within the cleaning category. This costs around £5 but lasts for ages. I've had a good few jobs from Gumtree, it's one more way to advertise and I never see the competition on there! When advertising on places such as Gumtree always aim to offer a deal. For example; 'Any average sized room within a 10km radius of (your area) for £30.00.'

This will set you apart from the boring cliché business ads the customers see all day long.

Another huge form of advertising which has developed a massive stream of clients for me is Checkatrade; everyone has heard of it. Every month according to Checkatrade, statistics prove over half a million consumers use their site to find a tradesman in their area. There is understandably a process to get yourself onto Checkatrade and a price. But I can promise it will be a worthy process and a great investment for your business.

The process to become a member involves one of their colleagues visiting you at your home address to discuss your business, proving you have public liability insurance; registering you with trading standards and asking you for 5 previous customers you've worked for to get your services. Luckily for you you've already completed 5 jobs so those people will be more than happy to leave you the reviews needed for you to become a member.

I believe the membership is between £6-700 for a year, but this can be broken down into 4-5 monthly payments to make it more manageable. Other similar sites include 'trust-a-trader', 'ratedpeople.com', 'mybuilder.com'. I'm sure there's more, I haven't personally used any of the others above therefor I'll leave it to you to do your research and find what suits you best. Speaking from experience I have received more jobs from Checkatrade than most other sources of advertising. They give you the platform, you give your services.

Another form of advertising is flyers. You know, those annoying things you get through your letterbox almost everyday, yes them, they work. According to the Direct Marketing Association (DMA) as many as 79% of recipients either keep, pass on to a friend, or glance over the contents of a leaflet distributed item. It's worth considering flyers with money off vouchers are kept by 33% more by potential customers. 38% of flyers are kept for at least a few days and 13% are kept for over a week. Money off flyers are 50% more likely to be held for at least a week.

The secret to advertising with flyers is preparation. There's factors within a flyer which are often not taken into consideration. A flyer needs to be colourful with the information short and to the point - people engage more with pictures. Try not to be too cliché such as including the obvious 'no job too big or too small'. Aim to be original.

These points are worth considering when designing your flyer. I advertised a local ad in Facebook to source a graphic designer who was training who would design me a flyer. I gave her the text and included before and after photos and she got to work. This service cost me next to nothing and was done very professionally to a standard I would have not have achieved doing it by myself. I made them double sided and packed enough details to have the consumer ask more questions. I then used vista print.com, uploaded my own design created by the graphic designer, chose sensible paper quality and had 5,000 delivered for less than £100. There's a small local businesses offering the same service on eBay for a more competitive price - it's up to you.

The whole process including designing cost me £150. The amount of revenue I received from this technique was over ten times as much in value compared to the price of the flyers; for the jobs I didn't receive, it wasn't wasted as it created awareness. Even if I didn't get one job, to me it was a great investment, you are letting people know who you are. They may not book you on the first flyer or even the second 3 months later or the third by Christmas, but I bet you they will by the fourth.

According to the National Sales Association –

- 2% of sales are made on the first contact.
- 3% of sales are made on the second contact.
- 5% of sales are made on the third contact.
- 10% of sales are made on the forth contact.
- 80% of sales are made on the fifth contact!

Sometimes it just takes some work to close the sale. This is no different from flyers.

You need to continue to put your brand in their face, don't let them forget you. Can you remember the ad on TV? *"You buy one, you get one free, I said you buy one, you get one free"*. Or, 'Compare the market, compare the Meerkat?' When this first came on it drove me mad! But now I use it. It's like a song which comes on, you hate it, but you sing it.

This is like leaflet dropping, eventually they will have to call you if you persevere with it. Put out an advert on Facebook requesting a person who'd like to earn some extra cash delivering flyers for you, the going rate for a professional company to deliver flyers can be anywhere from £35-100 per thousand. If you could find a trusted person you could save yourself money, or even if you have a day free you could do it.

Another form of advertising which I would recommend is showing up in shop windows, with your business card or flyer that is. Get round to all your local post offices, newsagents, estate agents, off licenses, anywhere which will take your business card and put it in their shop window. Normally it's £0.50-1.00 per week, which is a good investment and cheap in the grand scheme of things.

There is are other forms of advertising which I touch on further along in the book, which I feel could be put to use further down the line - but I wouldn't recommend straight away.

- Radio advertising is an option; have your business broadcast over a local radio station, prices for this normally start at £50-100 per week minimum.

- Adverts in your local newspaper, again these are costly; if you aim to keep it up expect an ongoing bill.

- Placing your flyer or business card in all the local billboards, some of these are locked so you will need to contact your council.

- Another form of advertising is Google AdWords which I will go over in further depth in the following chapter.

There are hundreds of companies available all ranging in price who will use unique keywords relevant to your website for you to show up in google page 1. So for example if I used this service a customer would type in "Carpet Cleaner Sussex" and I would come up on the first page. This can be costly depending on what keywords used and has so many factors to determine if you reach page 1 consistently each time. It's worth looking into in the future once you are more established for this type of industry.

Personally, other than what I've mentioned earlier, I wouldn't begin to use radio ads, local newspapers yet or google SEO ranking for a business such as carpet cleaning. I'd focus more on personal touches by creating tailor made packages for your existing and future customers.

A great scheme I use is a loyalty card. Each customer is presented with a loyalty card on the first job and after 4 jobs; they receive a free clean of a room, or a flight of stairs. I have loyalty cards with my local car wash and curry house, I'll always go back to them just for the stamp as I know I'll be getting something free.

How I use to present an invoice to a customer was to make my own invoice, **we provide a downloadable one at www.entrepreneurs-platform.com**, I would then staple a business card in the top left and a loyalty card in top right. You could use your signature as a stamp to save buying stickers to use. You could also then get yourself some cheap plastic transparent folders, place the invoice in this with the relevant cards, plus a flyer to hand to your customer. Little touches like this go a long way.

Another way I consistently advertise is by sending out a thank you letter every 3 months to all my existing customers reminding them I am still around which includes a £5.00 money off voucher as an incentive to use me again in the future. The going rate at present is £0.54p for a second class stamp and roughly £5.00 for 100 envelopes. For £60.00 you could send 100 out. I book over £1000 worth of work from this method especially if you make the thank you letter seasonal. Alternatively, you can purchase 100 envelopes with stamps already on them for a discounted rate of £35-45.00 with free shipping from eBay sellers giving you a huge saving on this method.

CHAPTER

7

EXPANDING MY CLEANING BUSINESS

"Practice makes comfort. Expand your experiences regularly so every stretch won't feel like your first."
Gina Greenlee

So you've set up the business, it's been running well for 3-6 months. Clients are beginning to recognize you and your brand. They keep noticing you driving around with your sign written van and seeing your adverts all over the internet and on social networking.

So what's the next step? After 3 months of carpet and upholstery cleaning, I decided to invest £350.00 into another bolt on which would hopefully benefit the business, it made sense to add this bolt on as it is relevant and cost effective. The bolt on I added was general cleaning, end of tenancy cleaning and one off deep cleans - It worked beautifully.

The greatest thing about this bolt on is that it's a cheap investment, easy to market and there is a great need for it. Especially if you already offer carpet cleaning as you can sell it as a package. I went to a local supplier of cleaning supplies who I sourced online and purchased everything I could possibly require from mops to oven cleaning equipment.

I then created a new page on my website, which was simple as I had a WordPress based website and titled it general cleaning. I then researched other cleaning companies and looked into their prices and learnt all about what they offered in regards to cleaning, what was included, and their price structures.

After this I set to work on creating packages for my customers. For example; end of tenancy clean for a studio flat, end of tenancy clean for 1, 2, 3, 4 bedroom flats, with an extra surcharge for houses. I then created a price structure for the package above, but to include carpet cleaning and oven cleaning. Then an option to subtract oven cleaning, or carpet cleaning. I then updated my van sign writing to include end of tenancy cleans and updated my Checkatrade to do's and included I now also offered end of tenancy cleans in my description. I began including this in my listing when advertising on Facebook. Anywhere I had listed or was listing my services I now included end of tenancy cleans and general cleaning.

For one off deep cleans I charged a flat rate; for anything else the job was charged as a price job as oppose to hourly rate. A one off job price you will receive more as oppose to an hourly rate. For a 2-bedroom house end of tenancy clean without carpet cleaning or oven cleaning I was making £165.00. This took me 3-4 hours to complete, less than £10 in chemicals. If I had charged an hourly rate; I would have only made £33-44.

For a 2-bedroom house with carpets and oven cleaning I was making £300. This would take me 6 hours, prepping the oven when I arrived, doing the cleaning off the house, then the carpets as the dust from the clean would go into carpets, followed by clean of oven. If I had just charged an hourly rate; I would have only made £66-77.

With this bolt on in place I began generating more revenue. End of tenancy cleaning is a huge niche. Yes, I admit when I began, I knew nothing about cleaning other than tidying my house. But you learn - the first couple of jobs were iffy, but after those I began learning what the customers would and would not like.

Work took off and before long through this bolt on, I needed staff. I would price a 4-bedroom house end of tenancy clean with carpets and oven cleaning at £345 for 6 hours with 2 people, pay the other worker £45 for the cleaning, I'd take care of the carpets and oven, and walk away with £300. This was becoming a part of my daily routine.

It's very important to understand this bolt on cannot be added straight away; you need to become established, master one part of your business, then move onto another part. Like I mentioned earlier a jack of all trades is a master of none. If you try to do too much to quick, the business will flop.

According to Bloomberg, 8 out of 10 entrepreneurs who start businesses fail within the first 18 months – a whopping 80% crash and burn. A leading cause of business failure is over expansion which often happens when business owners confuse success with how fast they can expand their business. A focus on slow and steady growth is optimum. Many a bankruptcy has been caused by rapidly expanding companies.

Once I began learning what was needed to be done in each room, for example; a bedroom needed skirting and coving dusted, PVC cleaned, interior windows cleaned, light fittings, doors wiped. I set to work to create another page on my website titled 'What's included? Our task list'.

This page was for the client when they rung me, meaning instead of me spending an hour explaining over the phone what's included within the general clean, or the end of tenancy clean; I simply gave them my website to view themselves. The feedback began pouring in from the cleaning jobs, especially with the help of the £5 gift voucher incentive and before I knew it cleaning became second nature. It was so straight forward and complemented the existing business of just carpet cleaning perfectly.

The next bolt on I offered, was hard floor professional cleaning. There's a big difference between mopping a floor and professionally cleaning it. Yes, this is a bigger investment and you will need £500-1000 to add this to your business, but once added this creates a whole new stream of income. I noted other carpet cleaners offered this service and I was keen to offer it myself, after a few months of regularly paying of my existing business loan I was in a position to obtain another small investment - I used this to grow and expand the business further.

I purchased a "Numatic" hurricane hard floor cleaning machine with the cleaning wand attached plus the pads needed to work on all types of floors. There are other hard floor cleaning machines on the market - I purchased this one as it was recommended to me by Ashbys and the hard floor cleaning wand could be attached to my existing carpet cleaning machine to rinse and extract the floor. The machine was the most expensive followed by the wand, then the chemicals. The chemicals last well and once you have the machine - it's yours.

This machine was fantastic as it allowed me to strip, clean, seal, and polish basically all floors. The list included wood, vinyl, amtico, limestone, tiled and marble floors. For the full package of strip, clean, seal and polish I would give a price structure per square metre. Initially I was not sure how to price my services but I soon found by the square metre suited perfectly. I charged £5.50 for the full package per square metre, and most jobs I began obtaining were kitchen floors on average 20 square metres. The process normally took no longer than 2 hours to do a room of this size and I priced this at £110.00. 10 of these jobs equaled the money back I invested.

Another addition to the business you could include is exterior window cleaning. You can purchase water fed trolley systems which plug into a water tank or hose outlet and do it this way or have a water tank and an extended hose to it running to a water fed pole. The way this works is the tank in your vehicle purifies the water, removing impure elements and minerals, then runs it through the water fed pole and cleans the windows leaving them streak free because of the removal of certain elements in the water. It allows you too clean up to 65 foot on a pole with no ladder involved. The water fed pole system of cleaning windows has many benefits in comparison to the traditional way – the reasons are –

1. You're not working from heights. Since this was the biggest factor resulting in death and injuries within the work place, regulations have now been brought in to protect you.

2. Secondly, it is less intrusive on the clients since you're at ground level; your view will not be into their bedroom.

3. Thirdly, it is more cost effective and less time consuming using a water pole fed system since there is no hiring of equipment such as scaffolding and platforms. Timely because running up and down a ladder adds time; and because a water fed pole is just one piece of equipment as oppose to multiple pieces such as sponges, squeegees, and clothes which are required when using the traditional way.

I understand there are now a few methods of exterior window cleaning available. The traditional way could also be considered, but with taller story buildings -

health and safety regulations would not recommend you to climb a ladder over a first story building and not at all unless a suitable risk assessment has been carried out on the danger.

Another option of expanding is jet washing of patios, driveways, gutters and conservatories. This could also lead onto other options such as car cleaning. There are multiple types of jet washes available on the market; I would recommend a petrol generated one. More power, more convenience, less reliant on the customer having power source. You can purchase a huge baffled water tank for your van, even the ones which neatly fit over your wheel arch. Baffled is when they are made so that when you turn a corner whilst driving and the water stays the same level. This can be the water source for the jet wash.

Talking of jet washes, my next idea of expansion is car valeting. Everything interior of the car including seats, floor cloth, door cards, boot liner and ceiling cloth can all be cleaned with hot extraction of your carpet cleaner, and the rest cleaned with your cleaning products from expanding the business into cleaning.

But you don't yet offer exterior cleaning. If you were to invest in a jet wash and a water tank this is another direction you could take the business. Purchasing products such as rubber enhancer and cleaner for the tyres, alloy wheel cleaner, car shampoo, t cut and polish would give you the opportunity to undertake the cleaning of all cars. You could even purchase a machine polisher and offer the detailing and colour revamp of cars also.

The other option is to also purchase a mounted oven dip tank and offer professional oven cleaning on an individual basis. I touched on including it within end of tenancy cleans earlier, but not individually offering it as a one off service. There are two types of dip tanks available; gas and electric. Both required to be heated up prior to setting off for the job. They can be mounted into the back of the van and aid in the cleaning off all things which can be removed from the oven. These things include the back plate, racks, oven linings and gas tops. Whilst these parts are soaking you would be inside cleaning the oven.

Products and dip tanks and training can be purchased from *Dirtbusters.com* who are the main retailer of all associated products involved with oven cleaning and their own manufacturer of the products and equipment. If you were to spend £1000 on a dip tank package, and £400 on training, you could increase your income by offering this service as a single package. Just one single oven can be priced from £35-60 taking only a couple of hours.

See the great thing with a carpet and upholstery business is it can be morphed into a cleaning company. Once this is done you can then undertake basically every single element of cleaning available. But this example is all built on the initial foundations - the number one foundation being brand. You need to have a recognizable brand and not just your name as the business.

As you know I am part of all my local selling and advertising groups on Facebook. When someone puts a post out requesting a carpet cleaner, a general cleaner or end of tenancy cleaner, other companies comment to say they can do it. Within the comments there is me; House Proud Finish, Bob's carpet cleaning, Ryan's cleaners and Michelle's does cleaning.

Who will they pick?

Bob, Ryan and Michelle do not have a logo, a brand, a slogan, uniforms, a sign written vehicle, what do they stand for? People always complain as I'm always last to comment as I fail to see it immediately since I'm out on a job, but the first to get the job regardless. It's a point so many miss to incorporate into their business or should I say their current hobby for now, at least until they run it like a business. If I had named my business Ben's carpet cleaning I would not have been as recognized for window cleaning, car cleaning, oven cleaning, as I'm limiting my business outlook to just one element. House proud finish allows for expansion under the name, bear this in mind when considering a business name.

CHAPTER

8

FORMS OF MARKETING FOR OTHER BUSINESS VENTURES

"The consumer is not a moron; she is your wife."
David Ogilvy

In the previous chapter I discussed the best forms of marketing for a new business start up in regards to the cleaning industry. Understandably these marketing strategies will not work for every business, although flyers, a Facebook business page and loyalty card schemes can be used for any business start up regardless of industry, examples I used such as Checkatrade would only suit for tradesman. Since the aim of this book is to reach out to all small business start ups, I do not want to make it too specific to just what I have achieved with my previous businesses and my aim is too discuss all small businesses.

If your business is relevant to my cleaning company; then use the strategies I've written about to start with. But what about if you're business is the opposite such as an online shop or website? How would you get recognized and traffic to your site?

I've mentioned branding frequently throughout this book as I feel it's the number one priority to distinguish yourself. Using a brand logo and name is key. Being consistent with colours and font is vital. If your logo is blue, keep everything blue, if your font is in Ariel black - keep it this way throughout.

Before anything else, you need to design your product.

Whether you are the product or you have a physical product such as clothing or an online platform offering your services. You cannot think about marketing, funding or cash flow unless you have your product designed – otherwise what are you seeking funding for, what are you marketing?

Once this has been established, the next step is what audience you are appealing too and why will they choose you. If indeed you are designing an online shop, I will go over what to do next.

Firstly, think about if people need your product. Brainstorm and research your targeted audience.

- What age group are you reaching out too?
- Is your product for females or males?
- How many variations are you providing of your product?
- What sets you apart from your competition.

I would recommend starting by writing a mission statement or pitch. This would be a statement clearly explaining who you are and what you are trying to achieve with your product to explain to someone who knows nothing about you. Creating the mission statement will give you clarity and focus on exactly what it is you are trying to achieve.

Another term for a mission statement or pitch is a USP. A Unique Selling Proposition. If you have never heard of this it's basically a business term for explaining who you are, what makes your business stand out from the rest, and tells your customers what is so special about you and your services.

Designing your USP or mission statement begins with your target audience. As I mentioned above-

- What do you know about your target audience

and why do they purchase from the market industry you will be operating in?
- Are they looking for customer service, convenience, is your product a basic requirement?
- Is your product designed differently?
- Does your product provide a service which is scarce and not easily available?

After this research, you will be able to confirm a list of reasons why a consumer would purchase from you.

The next step in designing your USP is explaining what your advantages are as a business. We can all agree people have had bad experiences with some of the biggest recognized brands in the country. Only because these companies have a position in the market does not mean they are fulfilling their promises as a provider.

Create a list of your competitors and research what promises they are and are not fulfilling as a brand. If you can provide something your competitors are not, this gives you a great advantage offering your services over competition.

Think about something which is regularly missed within your market. For example; a mechanic. This is a personal example I will use relevant to me. A mechanic I feel for somebody who may have a lack of knowledge in regards to the workings of a vehicle, could be more transparent. Every dealing I have had with a mechanic has been one where I have never really known what is actually going on. I like to know what's going on so I know whether I am being ripped off or not. I understand some people just want the bill but I'd like to understand more about the breakdown in steps of what's happening, and exactly what I am paying for.

So I guess from that perspective in my mechanics USP, I would reach my customers on a level of understanding and promise to provide a full breakdown of work carried out and why, with a promise to be 100% transparent with my work. I would then explain how I would achieve this.

For example; I would title the job needing to be completed and have a template for each common job as to why its being completed, what would happen if it wasn't completed and alternative options if the customer did not want it completed. This would provide you with a competitive edge over your competition as although it may be a promise this industry is offering, it is not one which I feel is being fulfilled.

Once you and your brand is in place, you are certain on your product or service, you have a clear understanding of your target audience, designed your USP or mission statement explaining who you are with what you are trying to achieve and how you are different - Its time to build your presence.

CHAPTER

9

CREATING A PRESENCE ONLINE

"Leadership is about making others better as a result of your presence and making sure that impact lasts in your absence" Sheryl Sandberg

We've spoken about how to create a presence if you are a tradesman such as a carpet cleaner, or running a cash sales business selling pre-owned appliances. But how do you build a presence if you are looking to dominate the online industry.

Let's start by looking at some statistics.

According to the 'Local Consumer Review Survey published in 2012' - revealed 72% of consumers trust online reviews as much as personal recommendations from people.

Meaning a good website with a means to review for its customers will equate to an online version of word of mouth. Something to think about when designing your site, a verified feedback system.

According to 'Interconnected World: Shopping and Personal Finance, 2012' 61% of global internet users, use the internet to research products online.

Wow, that's staggering. If they have seen or heard of your product elsewhere - 61% are likely to search and end up on your website.

According to a poll researched by 'TMP Directional

Marketing' in 2011, revealed 69% of consumers are more likely to use a local business if it has information available on a social media site. This statistic will lead onto what we will discuss next, social networking.

According to the 'Google Mobile Movement Study, 2011' 88% of consumers who search for a type of local business on a mobile device call or go to that business within 24 hours. So make sure your contact details are everywhere.

3 in 5 small business owners claim they've gained new customers using social media.

The findings from a social media behavioral researcher, Tom Webster, revealed the top 5 reasons consumers follow Brands on social media:

1. Discounts and offers.
2. For the latest product information
3. Customer service
4. Entertaining content
5. Ability to offer feedback

Maybe it's worth noting this when developing your social media site and to incorporate those 5 suggestions.

It's plain to see the internet has steadily taken over. But I recently saw a statistic published within multiple blogs which suggests 90% of all internet business start-ups end in failure within the first 120 days! The reasons which suggest this, and I say this because I'd like you to avoid this are:

1. Many do not know the statistical probabilities they face
2. Many do not see themselves as being part of the failures or they wouldn't leap
3. Many are talked into things they are unprepared

for
4. Many don't know the basic concept of – "If you fail to plan, then you plan to fail".

Looking at the list above indicates that you should research your market as a must. Accept responsibility for when things go wrong, otherwise you cannot learn and move forward. Thirdly, do not rush into running an online business. The quote from Steve Jobs goes "Apple survived from not what it said yes too, but in fact what it said no too" Finally, plan, plan and plan some more.

Looking at the above statistics prove that there is in fact great potential to run a successful online business, the consumers are engaging and the numbers speak for themselves. The other side of the sword shows that many people are trying it, but 90% are failing within the first 4 months.

So how do we avoid failing in the first 4 months?

You need to treat an online business, like a REAL business. Just as much work, if not more at times, goes into an online business like any other business. It requires time, patience, understanding and versatility. If you think orders will roll in over night, think again.

Preparation is key. You cannot launch overnight. I wouldn't even think of launching your online product or service until you have statistically gained enough feedback and data to suggest it's a goer.

Dedicating enough time to your project. Just because the internet runs 24/7 and there are many smart applications which enable you to cut your work load, does not mean you can relax and assume everything is on auto pilot.

Forget about profit for at least the first month. Ideally you need to set a budget which will either provide enough for you to live for at least 3 months, invest from another business whilst still retaining its income, for example; 'bootstrapping', or keep your job until the online business is generating enough consistently to rely on its income.

Obtaining the right mindset. I have dedicated a whole chapter on mindset within the book. Attitudes such as - Get rich quick, I can work when I want too, I don't need a plan, I am my own boss so I can relax, will guarantee you will be within the 90% statistic. The term 'I am my own boss' with the wrong person can lead too non accountability because they assume it's just them. Yes, you will be your own boss, but the boss of you. Meaning you need strict discipline and holding yourself 100% responsible for everything you do.

Instant gratification. Those two words should not be entering your mind, or leaving your mouth for quite a long time. This advice is coming from me personally; you will not be able to pick the fruits of your labour until they are ripe. This honestly can take years. The first 3 months of my cleaning business I took no income. The following 12 months there were times when the business made no money some weeks. Understand this is a journey, not a race.

Persistence. Heard of the game angry birds? I read this on a blog some time ago. My son who is 4 is addicted to this game, I'm sure I am also. The creators of Angry birds who came to the spotlight from the invention of the game and generated over 2 billion downloads for their game, you know the ones who were an overnight success? No, no one is an overnight success. Three guys in Finland created a company called 'Rovio' and began creating video games.

From 2003-2009 they had created 51 video games, none which were successful. After 6 years the company was about to become bankrupt when the guys began going through other sketches they made trying to figure out what kind of game they could make to save the company - when Angry Birds was created.

Imagine if after those 51 times they decided to call it a day? The reason why I shared this story is because yes it's interesting, but I am putting into perspective of realistically what this will require.

My aim is not to put you off business, but to encourage you to work smarter and harder so when you decide to take the leap of faith into entrepreneurship you fall within the small percentage of business start ups who survive.

Let's go through methods of marketing and advertising online.

CHAPTER

10

FREE WAYS TO MARKET YOUR PRODUCT OR SERVICE

"Creativity is intelligence having fun" Albert Einstein

Once your website is built offering your services or product, no one will know about it unless you put the time and effort into marketing and advertising.

Marketing and advertising does not have to break the bank. First I am going to begin discussing free ways to drive traffic to your site to market and promote your product and service, then I will discuss the money ways which produce a good ROI.

Blogging.

Producing relevant and frequent blogs on your website which discuss your niche is a game changer in regards to driving traffic to your website. Why? Customers typing your name into their browser is the audience you already attract through your brand and name. But how does blogging appeal to a separate audience not looking for you initially, but land on you through your blog. Think about how many pages are on your website, 4? Maybe 5? Once the information is set on those pages, it's unlikely to be updated for a while right? Blogging is different; every time you write a blog either daily, weekly or monthly, your website flags up on the google ranking and helps rank you better in the search engines by showing your site is active with new content.

Another reason why every time you write a blog is good for your site is because this also contributes to promoting your product through social network sites. As it enables the user to share your content. Your blog may be in line with what your business does, but if it has variation and not entirely specific this will generate a whole new audience who will then land on your site. Once the user lands on your page it creates an opportunity to turn traffic into leads. How this can be done is by creating a call to action free offer when the user visits. What I mean by this is offering free eBooks, articles, fact sheets, free trials in exchange for user information. So the visitor lands on your page through a shared blog or a blog which shows up on google, your visitor sees the call to action being maybe a free eBook, the user clicks on the eBook to read or download which then requires the user to input their information which allows you to send frequent offers to the user via email.

This is huge. Because a blog post can continue to generate traffic even if it was published years ago. Have you ever typed into google for example where is the best place to visit in America? A blog comes up in the search engine results, you click on the link and it's a really helpful post about great places to visit in America. It was dated 2011 but nevertheless its great content and still very much relevant too now.

What this does for the owner of the site is generates massive traffic to their site. Their actual website may in fact be about a nail salon. But the owner fancied writing about what to see in America and now someone has landed on their nail salon page to read the blog and is booking to have their nails manicured next week! Brilliant.

Blog commenting

Blog commenting on other people's blogs also works very well. If you are set up as your company and you are frequently blog posting on other people's blogs. Readers will become curious as to who you are - this will increase the likelihood of them landing on your page.

You could also set your blogs to group blogs. Where the public can also blog post on your blogs!

Cross Promoting

Another free way to promote your business is through cross promoting. An example of cross promoting is say where you run a graphic design company online and you have a recommendations page built within your website which recommends a provider who builds websites. In return, the business who builds the websites promotes your graphic designing on their website. Cross promoting is more explosive when the businesses you are cross promoting with are relevant to the services you offer.

Google+

Google+ is a great way to promote your online presence. Google uses your information to create a web presence by ranking your images and text. Setting up a Google+ profile is quick, easy and free.

Networking events and clubs

Joining your local networking clubs is explosive. It amazes me how many people I come into contact with when I am visiting the barbers, on a job, shopping or talking to online. Once you drop into conversation that your beginning a new start up, you will be amazed who knows who. Networking clubs are the perfect place just for this. I may be speaking to my barber who has a sister who mentions to her husband and is the CEO of a huge company who would be interested in my services. Do a local search of networking clubs and sign up, majority are free or at most ask you to help provide referrals for other members in return for them to do the same.

Free giveaways

Free giveaways on your website or your social networking sites works well and generates overall traffic to your site. Incentives for traffic is a good return on investment. A free iPad, cash prizes or tickets to a show. Create a contest on your social networking sites with an easy question needing to be answered, the user will comment, friends will see their friend comment, then comment, before you know it everyone is participating and potentially landing on your website.

Twitter

Twitter is huge and should be used to your advantage, in 2014 Twitter was ranked the 9th most visited website in the world according to Alexa rankings, and the 2nd most popular social networking site.

How can you use twitter to leverage exposure?

- Tweet regularly, preferably using visuals such as images, related information and articles which are relevant to your niche.

- Users prefer visuals over text. Follow trends and hashtags which suit your business. If your business is a nutrition website providing nutrition information to clients, follow nutrition hashtags and trends on diet. This puts your business in the spotlight because you can retweet this content to attract more users who have similar interests. Any great content you notice, be sure to share with your followers. If your followers notice and also retweet, their friends will also see.

- Create a hashtag - your own personal hashtag. For example; if you had a forex currency trading business teaching newbies how to trade the foreign markets, you could create your own hashtag of your brand #Forexknight and you could also use this on Instagram which is a huge marketing platform. You could also design an Instagram template which is used every time you post on Instagram just add the relevant text to it every time. This creates consistency for your viewers and explosive brand awareness.

- Talk to your fans. I follow a number of well known business gurus on social networking, some reply, some do not. But I certainly warm to those who take the time out of their busy schedule to reply to my frequent comments. This goes back to personal touches which I discussed earlier on. People remember how you make them feel, not always what you say.

How can you use YouTube?

If you are creating daily or weekly blogs, why not do a video version on YouTube? For example; if your business is nutrition, or you are growing with your fans in regards to diet plans, how about you upload you directly doing the diet plan throughout your day? Showing your customers how to meal prep. Or if you have developed a product why not show it off in use on YouTube or show multiple variations of your product? Or sneaky previews of what's coming next.

A weekly or monthly newsletter is vital to consistently reach out to your customers as a reminder. This could contain freebies, up to date information about you and your products or services; incentives, eBooks and links to articles or blogs.

These are just some of the brilliant ways to market and

promote your product or services for free. All this requires is consistency, patience, persistence and ultimately your time.

CHAPTER

11

PAID MARKETING TECHNIQUES WHICH OFFER GOOD RETURN ON INVESTMENT

"Everyone lives by selling something" Robert Louis

If you have everything covered on the free marketing side, now its time to look at what you can do with a budget to get the best return on your investment.

The ways I used which worked for my appliance business were the local directories to advertise. The appliance business I run is a tight localized niche therefore local advertising worked great. If you are selling a product which involves the community; I would strongly suggest using directories such as Friday-ad or Gumtree.

You can post for free on these directories, although there is a paid option which increases exposure and could potentially lead to a quicker turnover.

Facebook campaign adverts work well. Facebook claims 40 million businesses now have a Facebook business page, out of those 40 million, an estimated 1.5 million are investing in Facebook ad campaigns.

Why are so many businesses investing in Facebook ads? Probably because worldwide Facebook claim to have over 1.44 billion monthly users, with 890 million joining everyday and 5 users creating profiles every second!

Statistics prove traffic to Facebook is at it's highest between 1-3pm. Worth noting when producing a campaign advert. The split between male and female is almost a 50/50 split.

So how can you create a successful Facebook advert? From my experience, visual over text is more beneficial. Even taking statistics and probability out of the equation, I know I would much rather see an interesting image as opposed to 2 paragraphs of text, that's a no brainer.

Targeting the correct audience which is relevant to your niche. Again, it's a no brainer, but targeting 16 year olds when you are offering the opening of your new pub down the road, probably will not result in many sales.

Why do people actually want to click on your advert? Are you doing the classical cliché business speech? 'The best barbers in town' We are not still trying that one, are we? How about 50% of your first hair cut? Barbers is a picky industry, once you've got them, their yours! I know I would click on a Barbers advert offering 50% off.

If you are offering a coupon or incentive, make the reward easily accessible. If I am beating around the bush to get my 50% maybe ill just leave it.

As mentioned briefly earlier which works is Google ad words. According to a survey carried about by 'Wish pond' online, businesses receive £2 for every £1 they spend on Google ad words. An interesting fact which is slightly irrelevant – "Insurance" is the most expensive google ad words keyword. Costing on average £54.91 per click!

Another interesting fact – according to Google Investor Relations, 97% of googles yearly revenue is generated through advertising! Adverts created which are placed within the top of the search results receive 10 times more traffic than adverts placed in the side bar of the search results.

Google ad words are brilliant, these work hand in hand with ensuring your website has good SEO (Search engine optimization). Spend some of your budget ensuring your website is being ranked higher than your competition and you are indeed showing up in the search results.

I believe you should have a percentage of your marketing and advertising budget purely set aside for just innovation with trying new things. If Facebook advert campaigns work and Google ad words then great, but allow 5-10% of your budget to invest into things which may or may not work. I am only suggesting methods I have personally used which has increased presence, we know these work from the statistics. But how about venturing out into the darkness and trying crazy ideas to market and advertise your product or service? A business is either going forwards or backwards, do not rely on just what you know works, when there potentially could be even more possibilities to explode your brand awareness to your customers.

Another great way to spend the budget available for marketing is free incentives for your customers. Give stuff away! Tickets to a show, branded clothing, spa days. Begin a competition, once an incentive is involved, momentum will build and friends will tell friends.

Also worth noting when dealing with customers, it's vital that you take all of their details. I didn't put this into play for the first few months of the business, I just took first names and addresses. Depending on whether your business is person to person, or online - It's really important you get the customers full name, full address, phone number and an alternative number if possible, and an email address.

The reason being is you need to build up a database of clients. If you have the customers number in a database and not just some random text from 3 months ago, you can easily contact them offers every few months to remind them you still exist. As mentioned earlier if you have the customers email, you can make a template or a newsletter of an email offer, and forward it too all your customers which produces great awareness.

I appreciate this is obvious, but manners and good grammar and spelling go a long way. No slang, always say thank you, kind regards, many thanks at the end of every message. Make them feel very appreciated, and show how grateful you are for their continued business.

CHAPTER

12

CHOOSING BANKS AND ACCOUNTANTS

"Wise people learn when they can. Fools learn when they must" The Duke of Ellington

You need to have other important factors of the business in place. A business account is important, you do not want your personal and business incomes and expenses becoming confusing. This needs to be set right from the very start.

So who do you choose? Is there even a difference? Yes, of course. Such as the free business banking for 18 months with certain branches. If you have had a personal account for some time with your current bank, they will understand you and your finances therefore this heightens your chances of obtaining credit if you wish to expand your business in the future.

Speak to your branch and ask for a meeting to discuss opening a business account. Understand that although you may have a personal account with your current bank, this does not necessarily mean you need to go with the same bank for a business account, but discussing their rates and structure is a good start. The actual procedure of opening a business account is simple and is all over and done with quickly, but please do not rush it. Once this is in place you then have an account number and sort code to place on your invoices and you can then begin to pay for everything with your business card to provide a paper trail.

Another benefit is you can pay all your earnings into this account, then decide what you'd like to pay yourself to your personal account every week or month by BACS bill payment. If you are going down the sole trader route initially that is, paying yourself through a limited company works differently, we will talk about this in the chapter 'Sole traders and limited companies'.

Let's go over different factors to consider when choosing a bank. I think a priority for me would be online and telephone banking. Us entrepreneurs are very much on the go therefore require portability in regards to our banking. I pay for a lot of my services via BACS payment, a quick and simple online transfer which is an available option for me through my bank. Having an online and telephone option is crucial for the everyday entrepreneur.

Fee structure. This is really not given half as much attention as it should be, especially when you have just been enticed into a free 18 month banking perk. Do you read those terms & conditions? No, I tend not too either. I just look at the big fee I am billed at the end of every month. Seriously, check the fee structure for when you do online transfers, cash withdrawals, paying a person, depositing cash and cheques and so on of what you will be charged.

Thinking of borrowing money? Well its likely you will be, or at least will need to in the near future, especially if you are looking to expand. Good debt is not bad idea; if good debt makes you wealthier than before then go get yourself some debt! Bad debt is grabbing yourself a car on credit when you have a car which is just fine!

Trends in lending according to the bank of England put Santander, Barclays, HSBC, Lloyds Banking group, Nationwide and Royal Bank of Scotland at the top list in regards to obtaining money. Statistics show in the second quarter of 2015 that small businesses have an

80% success rate in securing finance and medium businesses 90%.

More lending facilities have been approved in 2015 compared to 2014. BBA.org.uk shows the first quarter this year alone saw 35,000 small business loans approved! This figure is huge, just thinking about that figure is making me want to set up another business!

Believe it or not, lending can also come down to your postcode! So if you are refused, maybe it is time to make a move! I'm just kidding, but it is worth considering.

Different banks offer different interest rates which are variable based on the size of your loan and term required. Do seriously think about it when applying for a loan to get the exact amount you need, I don't mean to tempt you to borrow more, but when I first started I took out 3 loans in 18 months.

If I had taken out one loan - but larger; I could have received a much better interest rate and less interest overall for the term! This is where a strong business plan comes into play of your exact intentions and forecast for year 1,2 and 3. This will enable you a clear view on financing and allowing you to see how much you really need and at what point.

The main thing to remember when choosing an account is comparison, rates and fees, long term forecast and benefits offered and to give yourself time. If you can remember this, you will have no problem choosing what you need.

Have you thought about an accountant long term, I know I have mentioned initially not needing one right away; but choosing a reputable and knowledgeable accountant is probably just as important as choosing a member of staff! They almost need to act like a business partner and be competent in business skills and demonstrate to you how they can benefit you. Ideally I would look to meet at least 3 candidates so you can compare the three.

Check to see the candidates you are meeting are indeed regulated by a professional body and carry indemnity insurance which covers your business against any losses for bad advice given.

Testimonials and personal recommendations go far. Again, it comes down to word of mouth. If you have anyone within the family or your circle of friends who are also involved in business, maybe ask them for a recommendations of a reputable accountant.

Obviously the costs saved need to be greater than the actual cost of the accountant. Similar to a member of staff, there is no use employing anyone to do anything if it is not making or saving you money in one way or another. Be up front and to the point "What are your fee's?", "How will you bill me". Accountants have different price structures and invoice differently. Some charge yearly, others monthly and some on a one off basis.

People automatically assume an accountant just files tax accounts on their behalf. This really is a small percentage of what a good accountant can do. A good accountant can help sell shares within your company if you are a limited company, they can also help raise funds via crowd funding and angel investing. They can point you in the right direction with grants, give you information on tax relief schemes, business rates, and ultimately help you on how to avoid paying what you should not be paying.

Something to also think about is how engaging the accountant is. It obviously comes down to your needs and where you are within business. If you are a new start up with not a great deal of knowledge in regards to business, an engaging accountant who you can be regularly in contact with and provides frequent help is what you will be looking for. One who will proactively engage with you, to see how business is progressing. This is why I recommend to meet with the accountants to see how they match up to what you are needing. Understandably you will be sharing information so trust is key.

Location in regards to an accountant is not really as it once was. They would need to be within a short journey to meet and discuss your business. But with new developments such as cloud accounting - location is not so much of a factor now. Everything can be shared and worked with over the computer and internet connection. If you are restricted in regards to travel, or rural in regards to location, maybe an online accountant would suit you better?

Now if your clued up, understand the concept of income and expenses, you will not need an accountant right away. Simply having a folder of invoices and a separate one for all your expenses is more than enough to hand over to a qualified accountant at the end of the year for them to arrange and file on your behalf. I thought when I first started, I needed an accountant right away as a must, this is not always the case and depends on the sector and complexity of your new business.

The only reason I feel you'd need an accountant right away is for advice on setting up. For example, leasing and finance can be 100% offset against your earnings! Equipped with this information I now have my business vehicles on lease prior to this I paid for vehicles in cash. I was always recommended to lease vehicles, as oppose to buying outright, little tips like this are great advice at the start.

An office? From a new entrepreneur's perspective, not too sure on this one. Maybe years ago I guess as a large corporate business requiring many facilities and people around you, a block of offices would suit very well and would be a good investment. But a single entrepreneur setting up a business? It's your call - I feel all we really need nowadays is an internet connection.

We can connect through Skype, Face time, Periscope. We can even complete university degrees with our lecturer via online connection! Flipping the coin and looking from a potential staff's perspective, if I was looking to join your team and the work load was office and computer based, working from home is more attractive to me than in an office block! I feel it comes down to what business you are in fact looking to begin, if it involves fulfilling many orders yourself with physical stock, running multiple tasks which involves physical filing and storage, a location where regular clients visit, then maybe an office would suit you well. But I wouldn't be thinking about it just yet unless you meet the criteria for the points above.

CHAPTER

13

DO I NEED STAFF?

"A single arrow is easily broken, but not ten in a bundle" Proverb

This is a big question, and one which maybe is too early to be asked just yet. This book is aimed at start ups, but since you may refer to this book further down the line for pointers, its worth mentioning.

What to do when you need an extra pair of hands?

Do you employ or hire self employed workers? Immediately I'm screaming self employed from an owner's perspective - but there are more factors involved than just hiring someone on a self employed basis.

Such as how often they will be used, for what work and the nature of your business. Understandably temporarily hiring or sub contracting someone on a self employed basis is much easier for you. You do not need to take care of their tax or national insurance deductions and also do not need to pay a NI contribution as an employer for them. No holiday or sick pay is involved, no long contracts, no reporting to HMRC at every pay day, no long streams of paperwork, redundancy pay and more!

The downfalls of using a person to do your work on a self employed basis?

They cannot work a set amount of hours consistently

and frequently such as a contract or used basically every single day of every month of every year. HMRC will become wise to this and automatically class them as employed and allow them the employed rights. Hiring on a self employed basis means they do not represent your business or your brand, as they can easily switch to other businesses whilst working for yours.

There is most certainly something rewarding about seeing employees wondering around who represent your business and brand. A self employed contractor who you have hired in, unless they have been trained prior, will not learn like an employee will. An employee is majority of the time a consistent person on set hours with a contract in place who will eventually mold and become hopefully part of the growing business.

Whereas on a self employed basis they will miss this. A self employed person can substitute themselves with an alternative worker if one day they cannot make it to work. Meaning you could have any Tom, Dick and Harry. You would be using the PAYE system to pay your employees (Pay as you earn) if the weekly amount is over £112 for each employee. Below I have created a simple table showing some of the benefits of using a self employed person in comparison to an employed person. I would look to seek advice from your accountant and/or HMRC in regards to the rules and regulations further around this!

Employee (advantages)	Employee (Disadvantages)
Employees represent your business	Employees need benefits such as holiday/sick/maternity pay
Job security allows the opportunity to pay a potential cheaper hourly rate	Paychecks need to be paid regardless if business is slow
You are in control of their work quality and if the work load increases, you can rely on them	More paperwork is involved, contracts, payroll requirements etc.
You can consistently delegate regular tasks to your employees allowing you reassurance	You are responsible for any training required for your employees
Your employees learn with your business and become part of your business	You are responsible in deducting your employees Tax and NI contributions
Employees hold it together whilst you are away	You will need to report to HMRC for every pay check given

Self employed (advantages)	Self employed (disadvantages)
Although the rate you will pay will normally be higher, overall you will save more as you will not be required to pay holiday/sick pay	Quality of work is not guaranteed since they operate under their own terms
Flexibility. If it doesn't work out, use someone else. You can keep going through them until you find a match!	Mix and match involves the chances of a bad subcontractor resulting in a damage of your reputation
No training involved, you can hire someone who already holds the relevant experience for the job to use	No loyalty to you or your company, they do not represent your business which could act negatively.
They are responsible for their own tools, equipment, permits and licenses.	They operate under their business name, not yours. The brownie points goes to them for completion.

CHAPTER

14

ENSURING PAYMENT IS RECIEVED

"It's not your customer's job to remember you. It is your obligation and responsibility to make sure they don't have a chance to forget you" Patricia Fripp

I have touched on a method I used in regards to the cleaning business on how to ensure payment is made by using a simple signature from the customer to agree to the terms of recovering money within the 'cash flow' chapter. This is just one method. Although it is a good method; it doesn't guarantee you payment. The client could sign against this and still avoid paying - which could result with you pursuing legal action.

Although you may get your money back, this is a tiring process regardless. Putting a plan in place in regards to cash flow, for any business, especially a small business, is vital. It is understandably the more boring part of the business plan, but a plan of action in regards to payment collecting could save you hundreds if not thousands in the future.

Let's go over a few methods and musts when collecting money. Firstly - I would recommend dedicating either a paragraph or a page on your website clearly detailing your terms and conditions. Not just for payment, but generally how you will act as a company.

If your business industry is the sale of goods or services, a disclaimer would be appropriate to give the client a clear understanding or your do's and do not's and your responsibilities as a provider or seller. A disclaimer or terms and conditions will be as in depth as the goods and/or service you provide. Only you know based on your business what you feel is suitable to mention. Without a clear terms and conditions in place, you will set yourself up for future risks and misunderstandings. This is not even just in place to protect you either - but also the customer. Giving you credibility and giving clarity to your word as an agreement will also form good trust with your clients.

What I feel is mandatory to be included is:

- Payment collection conditions detailing how you will pursue the customer if they become a non payer.

- Complaints procedure

- Any guarantees or warranties offered

- Delivery procedures

- If relevant to your business a refund and returns agreement and a non delivered or damaged item procedure should also be included.

By law, on your invoice given, your business name and address should be included as a minimum. If you are taking the limited company route, your company registration number and registration address must also be included and if VAT registered this number will also be required. Invoice downloadable templates and terms and conditions can be downloaded for free on the Entrepreneurs Platform.

So other than including a terms and conditions on your website or invoice detailing the action you will take to pursue unpaid fees, what else could you do?

Communication is a must. If payment was due today,

give your client a friendly call to check all is in order. Follow up if the client was indeed happy with the work or goods supplied to check this is not the issue, obviously if it is, you know what to do. If it isn't, agree another date for the payment to be settled.

If you have included in your terms and conditions a set period of time in which you will pursue the client for overdue costs by way of legal action, make this clear to the customer if payment is still overdue. If this second reminder has not triggered the client to pay, the next step is borderline legal action.

I would suggest downloading our template on the Entrepreneurs platform which outlines that the client is in breach of contract and your terms and conditions clearly displayed on your site and/or invoice. This letter which if emailed or sent, will mention how you are now withdrawing your services and that you will be investigating legal action and holding them responsible for all fees incurred. This is something you really will need to follow through on, even on the chance of loosing more than you gave and sacrificing your time.

Another option, which depending on your business is worth thinking about, is breaking your services or goods into phases. Ask the client for a non refundable deposit to get you started and then price the phases individually. This means the client will be required to pay for the previous phase in full before being able to begin or receive the following phase. This allows you to not risk your time and work on the hope of being paid, if the client does not follow through, you are paid up to date for past work.

CHAPTER

15

PROTECTING YOUR IDEAS

"Think you can, or think you can't – either way, you are right." **Henry Ford**

Protecting your ideas is vital - a casual conversation about a brilliant idea could turn into competition. Laws surrounding protecting your ideas vary from country to country. I will discuss the UK since this is where I am based, I understand the US has their own rules in regards to copy writing, trademarking, passing off, patents and contracts.

Understand that you eureka light bulb moment may have already been designed or discovered and put to work. A simple search within the UK on the 'Intellectual Property Office' online will allow you to search for anything similar to your idea. If it doesn't exist, brilliant! Time to get to work on patenting your idea! If your idea is the sales of items such a photography, pictures and art, your work is already protected under UK Copy wright laws, and if you are producing your own articles and literature this is also protected too - but worth registering. I will go into greater depths about copyright shortly.

Patents, how easy are they, what would class the use of one, and how much are they?

There are two options in regards to obtaining a patent. You can file one yourself, or use a patent agent to write up and file one on your behalf. Filing one yourself understandably is more cost effective and will initially be approximately £200-300. Using a patent agent is far more expensive and to hire one will cost you £3-4000 or more. The process for patenting can take up to 3 years to finalize, alternatively there is a fast track system which takes up a year, for the same price.

Drawing and designing a patent is not as easy as it sounds - I would recommend using a patent attorney for this and for legal reasons. Your invention and design needs to be fully protected, the wording needs to be perfect and the idea fully explained.

The initial application for a patent protects your idea for 12 months allowing you to then discuss your idea to obtain potential investment, feedback and deals within the industry, this can be extended, but is costly. But because you are given the 12 month's period initially, you can then decide after 12 months whether to pursue your invention.

After 12 months you can apply for what is called a PCT. PCT stands for "Patent Cooperation Treaty". This is an international patent application which protects your idea within the UK plus 160 countries. A PCT application can cost up to £5,000, if extra literature and material is required this figure could be more. Other applications which you could consider is an EPC, which stands for European Patent Convention. This protects your idea within the majority of Europe.

A patent really is for something such as the ideas behind your product, how it works, how it is designed, what it does and why. A patent would only be granted if you have thought of a new idea, an improvement on an existing idea, or a combination of existing ideas.

Once any application has been accepted, it gives you the ownership of your design and allows nobody else to create something the same or similar, and prevents them from marketing or selling your item without consent. From a commercial perspective, a potential investor or business backer knowing you have a patent pending and a date from which you filed, is a good to score brownie points.

Now you have some more knowledge on how to patent your product including the estimated cost initially and why you would obtain a patent - Let's move onto a registered Design. These are the designs you see with the small "R" next to it.

Registered design

A registered design is really what the title says. It protects the external shape and design of the product. You can include much more, such as lines, contours, materials, texture, patterns and more.

Considered a lower version of a patent, since its based more on the design as opposed to how it works, your design can be protected within 28 countries of Europe. European registered designs allow protection for up to 25 years, with renewal needed every 5 years. Something which you would see everyday which has a registered design would be a Cadburys chocolate wrapper, or Walkers crisps. In the UK, to register your first design would cost £60, designs after this are £40 each.

Trademarks

Next up are trademarks. Trademarks are a powerful way to protect your logos, symbols and names of your products or business brand. Within the UK you are protected under a term called "passing off" - Which I will discuss later when I speak on Limited companies. Passing off is using the same or similar brand, business name or product and calling it your own. So although there is a certain form of unregistered protection available, registering a trademark is far more powerful.

A trademark needs to be individually filed within each country you wish to have it registered within unless you obtain a CTM, a Madrid system, or something similar and they last 10 years, which once renewed will remain active indefinitely. As of July 2014 you can apply for a CTM which gives the owner of the trademark overall protection for all Europe's 28 states. Other applications which can be applied for is the "Madrid system" which allows you to register your trademark in 92 countries.

Even if your trademark is unregistered, the trademark symbol can be incorporated into your design, brand or logo. Whereas a registered design does need to be registered prior to using the "R".

Other ways to protect your work is copywriting and NDA's (non disclosure agreement)

Copyright

Copyright is automatic under international laws. If you for example have a document created by you which shows the date and time in which it was created and send this document to another person who claims it to be theirs, you have an earlier date in which it was created. As long as you can prove the document was indeed created by you, you have protection this way regardless.

Using a watermark or a copyright deterrent such as "copyrighted material" placed on all your work will deter potential thieves from claiming your work.

Gimmick or not, you can find third party copyright companies online who will allow you to send them your work which registers it with them. What this does is basically provides added protection for you because you have a company who can vouch for you on the date you sent it. Websites such as *www.protectmywork.co.uk* allow you to copyright songs, photo's, logo's, graphic designs, websites and any other creative works. You receive a unique reference number and certificate for each piece of work registered with them, you can use their logo on your work as a theft deterrent, a free affidavit (a written statement confirmed by oath or affirmation, for use as evidence in court) and your work is registered under copyright in 168 countries. So if you really want to go even further, you can use a third party company to register with.

Non disclosure agreements

Other ways to ensure protection on your ideas, information, knowledge, content and designs when discussing with another party is an NDA (Non Disclosure Agreement). An NDA form is created between at least 2 parties, who wish to share information either amongst each other or as a one-way communication, but helps protect the information from being shared with anyone else other than the parties involved. It's one of the easiest legal documents available to people wishing to share information.

Other names for an NDA form would be a confidential disclosure agreement, a proprietary agreement or secrecy agreement. In the need for the other parties to understand a business concept, have access to information to help design a product or the content of a book to proofread and edit, a NDA form would offer protection to the owner of the information.

It's worth considering prior to disclosing any information regardless how big or small you may feel the information is, to consider an NDA form before, not after when discussing your idea with another person.

CHAPTER

16

HAVING THE RIGHT MINDSET

"Happiness has to do with your mindset, not with the outside circumstance" **Steve Maraboli**

I feel it's only right to touch on mindset. Everything for me is down to my mental state. How I choose to eat, how I communicate, what I will and will not do and how far I am prepared to go is how my mindset is on the particular day.

Sure, I have bad days - or should I say bad hours. I use to have bad months, I gradually got this down to bad days and now I only have bad hours. I honestly cannot remember the last time I had a consistent bad day. How come I only have bad hours now and not bad days? Because I am more in tune with my mental state, I recognize the signs and have learnt how to pull myself out with methods I use all the time which I will talk about in this book.

Naturally with the way life goes you will experience bad days, but I have learnt how to pull myself out quicker than I could before, to limit this to only bad hours.

How have I done this?

Through embracing the bad months or days, self reflection in those times and most importantly not viewing the bad hours as indeed bad; and choosing to embrace those times more than the good. You will learn more from a difficult time than you will ever learn from an easy time.

A huge proportion as to why we have bad days is simple correction. There is no bad with good, no joy without pain, no good luck without bad luck. As mentioned before, you cannot have a straight line upwards to happiness and success.

When I was trading currency on the foreign markets, I always looked at the charts as a way of life. The chart would shoot up say 100 points, but would need to come down a further 30 points before continuing to shoot up another 80. If you could allow for the come down of 50 points or the bad days, would you be less worried about when it was going to happen? If you could look into the future and know when you were to have a bad day, would you put things in place to make that day easier?

Should we just accept that we need this? As oppose to fighting it, and embrace it? Instead of categorizing yourself as, 'I am feeling bad today' maybe try asking, 'Why do I feel bad today?' or, "What can I do to feel better?".

Am I surrounding myself with people who are contributing to my bad days? Am I listening to the wrong opinions? Am I procrastinating? Am I being productive? Am I trying to please everyone but myself? Am I being true to myself and who I am.

Most people are in their most happy state of mind when naturally things are going their way. When they've just landed a new job, when their friends love them, when they feel popular, when the bills are paid and they have £100 left over in the bank.

But how I see this is outsourcing your happiness to other third party factors. All the time you are outsourcing your happiness to things which you rely on to be consistent, when they become inconsistent, you will feel down. This is when you need to begin to rely on yourself for your own happiness not others, and learn the ability to trigger your own happiness.

You need to understand that mindset is everything to do with being an entrepreneur. I need to be honest with you when I say, this is going to be hard work. You really are separating yourself from society, from the normal, this is a big deal. 95% of this journey is mindset. Mindset controls doubt, fear, energy, versatility, reactions, beliefs. I am by no means saying you need to be 100% perfect prior to embarking on this journey, as the journey will make you and teach you - some lessons just need to be learnt the hard way. You are basically jumping off a cliff and building a plane on the way down, with no engineering experience.

You are a new born cub, who should leave the nest at 8 weeks, but you are venturing out at 4 weeks old. You are leaving the normal now, and you are no longer looking backwards, only forwards. Yes, its unknown, its blurry, your unsure, everything wants you to feel comfortable but desire to see what life could be, is far greater than the want and need to be comfortable.

You have decided to buy this book, because the 40 hour a week job working for your manager on a shop floor receiving minimum wage is just not cutting it, you have brought this book because you feel differently, you feel a calling, you feel you deserve more, and you do.

Life is exactly what you make it. People say this all the time, I hear it so much myself. New year arrives and everyone makes resolutions, most are forgotten by the end of January. People are creatures of habit, and its no kidding when I say life is gone in a flash. I guess my great understanding of ensuring my life is spent doing what I want to do comes from the loss of my father at 8 years old. I've always wondered where I gratefully receive my drive from, my determination, and I believe it stems partly from this event. This event from a young age has put into perspective of how serious it is where life is concerned.

Ask yourself honestly, do I want to work until I am 70 years old, or do I want to live? You see, entrepreneurship is not work, it's not a job, it's a lifestyle, it's truly living. You do not count hours, you go further, you push harder, since its for you. You are paid on results, not hours, therefore you invest more of yourself.

I often wonder if people put in the effort they put into making sure they do not miss the latest soap opera into accomplishing their dreams, we would surely have happier faces on Monday morning. Promise me you will not settle for safety? This book was not written as a gimmick, its just me, writing away. From person to person, trust me when I say, being free and living life on your terms is worth the jump.

What's the easiest and fastest way to bring happiness to the surface during hard times?

Gratitude.

Being grateful for what you already have. I know this sounds so simple and at times is so hard to acknowledge when nothing seems to be going right. But more is going right than you initially think. Sometimes I will be driving down the road in a blur, my mind is racing, I'm feeling overwhelmed with everything going on, then suddenly I see an ambulance racing down the road with its lights flashing. I begin to question myself, how could I be choosing to feel this way when somebody at this present time is sat in a hospital bed taking their last breaths. That's deep right? But its true.

Take a pen before continuing on through this book and

write down 5 things you are grateful for. This may be your health, your current relationship, your family, your vision, your arms and legs, your ability to read and write, your home, your job, your friends, even the hard times you have experienced. Anything and everything you are grateful for. Really focus on this list, feel every part of the list, try to picture your life if the things you had wrote were in fact the opposite.

After completing a list of things you are grateful for, now write a new list of things you wish you could change.

These things may be for example;

- becoming healthier in regards to eating better foods,

- joining a gym,

- loosing weight,

- quitting smoking,

- joining a networking group to meet new people.

Now break down the list of things you wish you could change, and give each thing a realistic goal. For example; I would like to loose a stone in weight in 3 months.

Just by simply writing this down, subconsciously creates a sense of productiveness. When I am feeling overwhelmed, I write it down. I think that I have so much to do, I'm so stressed because I'm so busy, when I write it down and visualize it, it turns out that in fact it isn't all that much and seems more easily manageable when its broken down on paper.

Now you know what you want to change, you've

written down and given yourself a realistic time frame - you are already in a much better state of mind. Now you have a reason, a purpose, something to look forward too and work towards. It's similar to wanting to go on holiday, you are always thinking about it, wanting to do it, but until you actually book it you cannot become excited or happy about it.

Write down exactly what you want to change and begin working on the goal to change it, this will give clarity and focus. It's important to look at this list every single day. To start with, especially if naturally you are use to struggling with motivation, you need to be reminded and kept on track. Looking at these goals everyday will hold you accountable, you wrote that list, you now need to do what you wrote.

Being true to your goals by working towards them, and completing them provides a huge boost of self confidence. Why? Because there are two main parts of your brain. The conscious and the subconscious.

The subconscious will do whatever your conscious tells it, it's the part of the brain which is use to doing what its always been told to do. Your sub conscious probably knows you wont loose a stone if you have tried before and failed to succeed. But if your conscious mind is continually reminding the sub conscious that in fact you are working towards the goal, you are making progress or in fact if you've completed it, your sub conscious mind will be shocked. It will begin to have faith, and develop the ability of recognizing that in fact goals are achievable and can be attained.

Once this connection has been established, the next goal or obstacle needing to be completed will be easier. Since your sub conscious now knows the last goal was completed, and that you are a badass, this one also can be too. This in return creates confidence, and trust me when I say, being confident is the key to conquering anything and everything you have ever desired.

The subconscious mind is very similar to a library. When you drive a car, it becomes second nature, when you eat, breathe, walk is all from memory of your sub conscious library of knowledge stored from previous experiences. You do not need to think when you do. Success and happiness can also be trained like this, its just starting and being consistent which is the key to training the sub conscious mind through repetition.

Once you are use to winning and conquering, it not only becomes addictive, you will learn to not accept anything less. It's about giving yourself the opportunity to do this, and it all begins with setting goals and achieving those goals, however small they may seem.

There is also the unconscious mind. The unconscious mind is a part of the mind which is not as easily accessible. Parts of your unconscious mind can become subconscious, then conscious, for example a childhood memory which has been surfaced by a trigger, but would have remained hidden without triggering. Your beliefs, opinions and what makes you who you are today would have been contributed from your childhood and library of unconscious memories. This is where financial intellect could have been developed.

If your mother and father did not have great control over their finances this may be contributing to why at every pay check you receive you have to spend every penny to make sure it is all spent. To why its irrelevant as to how much you earn, you never seem to have anything left. This can also work to the opposite too. You may have seen, felt, heard something when you were younger which has shaped your opinions today on how you feel about relationships, friendships - maybe now you religiously save every penny because you feel scared of feeling how you felt when you were younger.

This is similar to anchoring. Something I have worked on over the last year or so myself to feel consistently confident. Anchoring is when you can manually trigger feelings and thoughts in your sub conscious or unconscious mind. Let me give you an example of anchoring. I am no doctor by any means or a psychologist, these are just methods which have worked for myself.

When a phone rings, you feel compelled to answer it. Why? Of course you've answered the phone a hundred times before, and you have anchored the thought of a phone ringing to answering the phone through repetition and previous experiences. Here is another example.

You smell the smell of chips when driving down the road with the windows open from a local pub. You begin to feel hungry and it reminds you of a time when you were sat in a pub, eating chips. But not only that, you also remember exactly how you felt when you were sat at the pub eating and smelling the chips at that present time and begin to feel like it now.

Another example. You are sat listening to music you like, then suddenly, a song comes on you recognize. It's maybe a song you had with an ex partner, "your song" - and it brings back exactly how you felt when you hear the song. This is triggering the unconscious mind to feel exactly how you want to feel. This is called anchoring and can be achieved manually.

You literally can trigger your mind to feel however you wish it to feel in times of need. It works, I have used this method many times before. Yes, I was skeptical initially too. Sounds a bit silly I know, but trust me when I say it works.

Anchoring works basically by mentally tying a particular feeling such as relaxed and a calm state of mind, to a combination of triggers such as a visual (looking at a particular object), auditory (repeating a phrase out loud to yourself), or kinesthetic (squeezing your hand tight) anchor.

Naturally it requires time to accomplish this, but once accomplished, the anchor process can continue to be used over and over again. So for example; think of a time right now whereby you were so happy. Maybe you had just received amazing results from an exam you had completed, the time you first kissed your current partner, or how you felt on Christmas morning last year, a feeling where you felt so happy with everything

Now really focus on that feeling, where you were, exactly how you felt.

Once you really feel that emotion, it's at its highest, now think of the physical kinesthetic motion you want to use to anchor this emotion with. For example, if the emotion is the happiness you felt, you may squeeze your hand tightly and then say out loud to yourself "I am happy". Now stop doing it and switch your mind to think of something completely different, like your job you need to get up for tomorrow!

Keep repeating this process, over and over 5-10 times to create this anchor. Do not leave a day between repeating it, do it now.

Now, in a few days, try this anchor. I want to laugh, because I know this will work and you will say, 'Wow!' I can literally generate that memory of happiness just by squeezing together my hand and saying "I'm happy" whenever I like? That is the power on anchoring. I use this method when I am feeling anxious to remind me of a time when I sold my business and how I felt once I received the money, the words I use are "I am confident".

So I've touched on gratitude and anchoring. What else do I use to stay within a positive mindset? How do I continue to be productive, energized and motivated even on the bad days or hours?

A mixture of reminders, mind tricks and a consistent belief that something great really is about to happen. I also set a rewards for hard work completed. For example; I purchased a watch I always desired after 3 years in business. I'm not suggesting wait 3 years to reward yourself, but regularly give yourself a pat on the back. These rewards then act as reminders, I take a glance at my watch and it reminds me of why I brought it and the hard work I have contributed. I guess the watch acts as an anchor for me.

I also follow my progress with a daily diary - I look back on some things I have wrote in amazement at how far I have come, which in return boosts my confidence and reminds me on the journey I am travelling. I take lots of pictures of my results, money generated, figures and environments where I was most happy; to look through when I lose focus, almost like a happiness photo album.

I self reflect a lot - what I mean by this is I analyze my day and think about what I could have done or said differently. Self reflection and writing your thoughts down is a game changer. Just being self aware of your thought patterns and body language is first step to being open to change within yourself.

We all have an unstoppable, confident, risk taking part of our brain. Some of us find it easy to bring this to the forefront, others have this ability buried, or do not understand they have this ability as a way of choice. But I promise it exists, we just have to get use to using it more.

I want to go back to a time in my life when I was not confident, I couldn't communicate with others as well as I do today, I wasn't as enthusiastic and passionate as I am now. When I was 17, during working at the warehouse, I attempted to try a different industry. Believe it or not, its something I am involved in now - which is sales. I had to cold call on people's doors to generate sales for a double glazing window company. I use to be petrified, I'd knock and stand there silently. The house owner would ask me what I wanted and Id just stare at them not knowing what to say. It's funny looking back on it now; I was useless at selling.

The reason why I am sharing this story with you is because now I am great at it. Hey, did you listen to that, I just said I am great at it. Maybe I'm not, Woah! there goes the self doubt, but the belief I am, is what makes me confident enough to be great at sales. See, sometimes its just a matter of recognizing your thought patterns and adjusting them.

What other qualities are needed?

Patience is important as a visionary - it's something I am still working on. I have visions of how I would like things to be and I am set on exactly what I want, I don't want to wait, I want to be hitting them goals already. This is great as it drives you, but allow yourself some slack as this doesn't all happen over night.

A book like this, will help cut your learning curve and allow you to be better prepared and less overwhelmed. Time is important, I never feel like I am at work. I did not do any of my businesses based on hours, it was an ongoing project throughout - from the moment I open my eyes until the moment I go to sleep.

If you asked me how many hours I work a week, I couldn't tell you. Allow for the fact it is not going to be 9-5 or 10-6. It will be whatever you decide to dedicate to it. I always use a way to explain my business's as a newborn child, putting in the days and nights, giving the love and time, raising them with discipline and direction. It is very self satisfactory and rewarding watching something you have created grow, especially one day by itself.

You need to allow for mistakes, and failures. This is something I work on daily, I set high expectations for myself and feel self doubt when they are not done the way I imagined or things did not turn out how I wished. This is expected and again drives you meaning you have a better awareness of your present situation. But being to hard on yourself will not produce the results you need and will stop your productiveness. You need to be intentional with your time. It isn't about how many hours you do, but what you do in them hours, which counts.

CHAPTER

17

SOLE TRADERS AND LIMITED COMPANIES

"Kites rise highest against the wind, not with it."
Winston Churchill

Regardless of what industry you are entering to start your business - you will need to become self employed. This involves ringing HMRC (Her Majesty's Revenue and Customs). Once you've registered you will receive a UTR (unique tax reference number) and as a sole trader will begin making your own national insurance contributions; I believe monthly, quarterly and yearly are options to pay.

According to HMRC standard national insurance contributions are class 2 – which is £2.65 per week. Class 4 national insurance contributions are issued on profits over £7,605 at a rate of 9% up to £42,475 and 2% thereafter. You will also be required to pay your own tax contributions. You will be required to pay 20% tax on income from £10,600-£31,785 and 40% tax on the income generated after £31,785 and 45% on income over £150,000. The standard personal allowance for 2015 is £10,600 which is what you can earn before being taxed.

As a limited company, things are not much different in regards to percentages. Your corporation tax will be at a rate of 20% for earnings up to £300,000. Above £300,000 your company will still be paying 20% on earnings. This new rate was introduced this year with the intention of reducing to even less over the next couple of years.

These figures may or may not have changed since this book has been released, I would always recommend talking to an accountant to get an up to date rate on national insurance contributions and what you should be paying as a sole trader. If you are going down the accountant route when you first start up, they can advise and help with this.

The differences between the two?

Being a sole trader; you are 100% responsible for everything to do with the business. You and the business are one, so if the business runs into trouble, your personal finances could also be involved. As a sole trader - it's an easier set up with regards to accounting, less admin, less in accountant fees and you keep all your profits after tax and national insurance contributions. Depending on the business I'd normally recommend at least starting out as a sole trader, especially if you initially predict a low income - although there is no wrong or right answer.

Being a limited company you are separate from the company. You are treated as a director and employee of the company, therefor the company is a different entity. Meaning if the business runs into trouble, it doesn't affect your personal finances and you are more protected, obviously if you haven't made any personal guarantees against your assets that is. There is more administration involved, you will also need to register and legally submit annual returns to Companies House. Something else worth considering is withdrawing money from a limited company, this is not as easy as doing so with a sole trader. Taking money from the company needs to be formally recorded as a salary, dividend or loan.

When I established one of my limited companies I used

a third party company to take care of the process. If you undertake a simple search on google, you will find numerous companies who will submit your application to Companies House on your behalf. These companies also offer support, business accounts, accountants and more for a fee slightly higher than what it costs to register with Companies House. This process is much faster than using Companies House, normally taking no more than 3 hours! If you are impatient like me and want to see your business name on a certificate faster, I'd recommend using this option!

It is difficult for me to say which option is best, limited or sole trader, since both have their advantages and disadvantages. Limited companies do have a more professional feel about them, since there is more of a process and registration in becoming a limited company and more transparency it's seen as more legitimate and whole. Some companies will not work with sole traders, but maybe this isn't an issue depending on your business sector.

My appliance business never needed to work with anyone, which is one of the reasons why I kept it on a sole trading basis. The business had small outgoings, being a sole trader suited.

There is multiple accounting software programmes available on the market, which if you familiarize yourself with, could help reduce the costs when submitting your corporation or sole traders tax and deductions. I regularly use accounting programmes to submit my income and outgoings which acts as a great investment on time and money when handing over my tax return to my accountant at the end of the year.

Referring back to what we discussed earlier, your business name needs to be something which does not use your own name. As you want to create a brand which can expand. Being a sole trader it isn't required to necessarily register your business name, but ideally you want to be unique and not copy any one else's, at least not in the same part of the country you are in.

Being a limited company when registering with Companies house, you cannot register a business name which is already in use. Legal action could be taken against you under 'passing off' rules. Trademarking your business name prevents anybody copying it and allows you legal protection against anybody who registers the same name.

CHAPTER

18

FUNDING

"The ultimate measure of a man is not where he stands in moments of comfort, but where he stands at times of challenge and controversy." Martin Luther King, JR

We touched on funding briefly earlier, when I discussed my method of funding my new business start-up with the bank. I would like to now go over other methods - as I understand the bank isn't an option for everyone.

- Personal savings work as an option. If you have savings in the bank and it isn't exactly collecting much interest, this could be an option to starting your business. It means you could start potentially debt free, no interest, and it is convenient as it's to hand without long applications and questions. This term is known as 'bootstrapping'. Although this is a good option for you as it requires no debt or giving away equity within your company, it also carries financial risks and could stunt the growth of your business.

- Angel investing. Angel investing is seeking money through investors, in return they take ownership of a share in the business. They could either contribute towards the business, or be a silent partner. Very much how dragons den works. The disadvantage of angel investing, or investors in general, is the equity needed to be given. Initially this option sounds appealing – be careful not to give away too much of your company and lose the direction of the business in the process.

- Limited company. Being a limited company allows you to sell shares within your company to the public. This gives away a stake of the company in return for investment. Accountants can help with this.

- Friends or family. Borrowing from close friends or family may be an option for you. If this is an option, be sure to write a formal agreement or contract on how you will either pay them back, or what percentage of the business you are giving them. This makes it clear from the beginning and prevents any misunderstandings.

- Business start up grants. A simple search on google will reveal many business grants and start up loans available to you. These are a great advantage to you and some can be topped up further down the line to allow you to borrow more.

- Asset based finance. This is a method where you receive money against your assets you already own. For example; if you are a home owner, or a car owner, loans can be secured against these assets.

- Crowd funding. An online service where you pitch your idea and multiple people invest an amount. Some may invest £30 others may invest £1000. 1,000 people may invest a £1 each or 10 people invest £100 each. According to Wikipedia, the crowdfunding industry raised $5.1 billion worldwide for new business ideas. I would suggest using the business protection chapter for ideas on protecting your invention prior to advertising the idea on a crowdfunding platform.

Crowdfunding platforms available today include:

'Kickstarter' - Being the most popular Crowdfunding site to find funding for business projects. For an all or nothing model, which if the funds needed are not met you receive no funding, you are charged 5% of funds raised plus a 3-5% transaction fee. Kickstarter is a good platform for the highest traffic which equals greater visibility.

'Indiegogo' – Being highly flexible, allowing campaigns to be submitted worldwide, unlike 'Kickstarter' who just target the USA & UK.

On an all or nothing campaign – 4% of the funds of a successful project are set aside for 'Indiegogo' on a flexible funding campaign which allows you to keep the money raised even if the goal is not met, you are charged 9%. If the goal is met on a flexible campaign you are charged 4%. Additional transaction fees are 3%.

Other crowdfunding platforms include 'RocketHub' who charge 4% for completed campaigns or 8% for a campaign which has reached a percentage of its goal – with 4% transaction fees. Disadvantages include less traffic as oppose to 'Indiegogo' and 'Kickstarter'

What to consider when creating a Crowdfunding campaign?

I would personally attempt to create a pre buzz prior to marketing a Crowdfunding campaign. I feel its important to build a social networking and general presence if at all possible, prior to reaching out. If you can successfully create an audience before launching the campaign – you are already onto a winner since you have an enthusiastic viewer in the crowd waiting to invest.

Videos display your vision clearer than text. Focus on developing a detailed video explaining your concept and product and you. A personal storyline works well, go into depths on who you are, your background, and what it is you wish to achieve.

Ensure your website is complete. People may want to go further into you and your background prior to investing. A well designed website will give you the backing needed and professional touch required when reaching out to your users.

Other methods of funding -

- Credit cards and overdrafts. I would not personally recommend this myself, unless you can raise the funds reasonable quick to get the money back in the account. I'd recommend this more to top up the funds needed, for example if you need £5,000 and you have £4,000, to put £1000 on your credit card, and have the money back in from the first month's sales to save interest. Credit cards can be an excellent way to build credit.

- A second business. If another business you own is in a position to help with funding for another, this will again allow you debt free borrowing which also allows you more flexibility and control over your new business venture and 100% ownership.

CHAPTER

19

CASH FLOW

"If you just work on stuff that you like and you're passionate about, you don't have to have a master plan with how things will play out"

Time to talk about the Benjamin's, the cash, the dollars, the bread. You need to be financially literate and money organized when running a business. I always wonder how one can be on a good wage packet and career such as a banker, a doctor, yet have no money. This is due to lack of financially literacy.

Within society's education you are taught History, English and how to write a long essay's; but not how to juggle money and flip it into profit. Cash flow forecasting is a tricky thing when setting up a business, I feel it is almost impossible to estimate how much your going to earn within the next 12 months for a new start up.

Factors which will decide this is your expansion rate. If for the first 6 months your sticking to just one part of the business, it is likely after 3 months you will averagely be able to estimate what the following 3-6 months will look like, plus an increase based on your brand awareness increasing.

The main factor of cash flow is not to worry too much about how much you think you will earn in this next 12 months and focus more on building your product and paying who you need to pay without getting yourself in too much debt. Speaking from only my personal experience, this has not had a huge effect on me by not thinking of my projected income forecast for the next 5 years.

I feel if you take care of the weeks, the months tend to take care of themselves. For new start ups, pay who you need to pay first. My method was to put all my loan repayments and outgoings towards the end of the month. I would then add all my direct debits together, so for example they stood at £1000, I would then divide this into 4. £250 per week I needed to have into my business account, anything after this, was mine. With what was left over, I'd leave 10-20% within the account then pay myself what remained. This system may or may not work or be right for everyone, but since this book is about my journey to help you, I found this way to work the best for me.

- **Invoice quickly and collect payment quicker.**

My method was to print two invoices prior to the job, one for me, one for the customer. For my first 3 months of trading, this worked well, until I had a one of customer who I ran into problems with - a non payer. The customer had rung me the week before and booked me to make a visit and give the house a general clean, based on the size of the property, and how she had explained it to me, I quoted 4 hours for 2 people at £11 per hour. Making it an £88 job.

When we arrived, there was a folder of paperwork as thick as the yellow pages of extra things which needed to be done, in hindsight I should have ran a mile, but being eager and keen I stayed to complete. I explained we would be charging more based on this and she agreed.

It ran into an 8-hour job, plus materials making the quote £180. We made an agreement for her to pay the invoice via BACS transfer and left. A few days later, have you guessed yet. No money.

We were told she was not happy, even after we walked through the property with her. We allowed the client more than enough time to reach a decision whether she was happy with the finish, which she was, still no payment. Our hands were tied and we had no choice but to remain polite and professional. Through persistence and remaining polite we managed to recover £100 of the £180. Fortunately, this was my first and last experience case of non payment.

I had to find a better way of obtaining payment from my customers. So I went back to the drawing board with my invoice, and added a specific clause. 'Please sign on the dotted line if you have inspected our work and happy with our service………………………… Any and all fees incurred in recovering monies from unpaid invoices will be the responsibility of the customer'

I then ensured once any work was done, the customer checked and signed to say they were happy with the work and to pay recovery fees, I never received a single issue since. See once you have a signature, they can't leave bad feedback or not pay.

- **Do not spend out money on 6 month's worth of stock unless it's part of your initial start up lay out.**

So when I first started I did a big buy on loads of my chemicals as the loan I had included this. But I would never do it otherwise, I only buy what I need. So I would purchase one 5kg of carpet cleaning powder which would last me 4 weeks with my amount of jobs. I wouldn't purchase 10kg for 4-8 weeks because it saved me £2.00.

This is cash flow, not money off your shop. I live by a theory. I occasionally use a sun bed where if you purchase 60 minutes, you receive 10 free for example. But if it takes a person 4 weeks to use 60 minutes and it's cost them £50.00 so a saving of £10, but I go pay as you go and just pay £1 every minute, that saves the initial outlay for me of £50. With that £50 by the time the person who has used up their £50.00 worth, I could have turned that money into £500. Bulk buying is good in certain areas, but it straps you for cash until the product you have brought is sold. So be sensible, do not put all your eggs in one basket and have no capital left for anything else.

- **Make it easy for your customer to pay.**

What I mean by this, is give them a thousands ways, yes I was exaggerating then, but we can't let them slip.

Depending on what industry you are involved in decides which payment options to offer first and as a priority. For my cleaning company, cash was preferred. So I accepted this as my number one, followed by a card reader and thirdly BACS payment by online or telephone transfer.

If your business is an online business, this may be the other way round. Card payments will likely be your number one payment method, or PayPal, followed by BACS payment and maybe cheque.

There are loads of deals available online for a card reader and merchant service providers who will happily be the provider who take payments on your behalf for your website for an initial one off set up fee and monthly payment. A lot of my competition did not have card readers or merchants, and it is convenient for the customer and how can they delay if you're also offering this method.

Depending on your industry, the only time I would accept a cheque is if you have built a relationship with your customers and there is a level of trust. Cheque's can bounce and have issues which you really could just do without when there are many payment methods available to your customers before accepting a cheque.

Other options for payments could include biscuits and tea. I'm just kidding.

- **Regularly update, check and analyze your financial books.**

If I came up to you 6 months into your business and asked what your turn over was, what your profit was, and how much on expenses for each month the last 6 months, you should be able to tell me. You need to know where you are at, and where you are heading.

- **Do not miss payments, to any one.**

Stay on good terms with all your lenders. You never know if you may need an increase for expansion in the future.

- **Try to aim to obtain what you can on credit, finance and lease especially vehicle purchases and equipment.**

This can all be offset on your taxes and frees up cash. Don't go full steam ahead when first setting up, third party companies will be ringing you all day everyday when they catch wind of you first starting up trying to sell you this and that. Remember, the reason Apple done as well as it did, was not because of what it said yes too, but what it said no too. Be sensible.

- **Encourage repeat business.**

We spoke about this earlier, with loyalty card schemes and voucher incentives. With a loyalty card, voucher incentives and good professional service, they will never think twice of switching companies I guarantee it. Like I said earlier, I use a specific curry house, who isn't the best, but I love the loyalty card scheme as something free is coming up! Once they are on your side, they are part of you and the business, reward, encourage and promote.

- **Do not expand to quickly.**

One of the biggest reasons such a huge percentage of new start ups fail is because they tried to expand too quickly. I believe a trait of a successful entrepreneur is having a matter of urgency, but there really is a difference between expanding too quick, and then being sensible and logical.

It is all a process and although you may see other businesses already where you want to be, remember what is happening with them is the event, what they did before this event you now see, was the invisible slow process. Do not be knocked off the track of patience because of comparison. The only person you need to be comparing yourself too, is who you were yesterday.

- **Prioritizing.**

As a business owner, you will be regularly wearing more than one hat and being more than one person. Some days you may be an accountant, a salesman, administrator writing up letters. You will be juggling tasks, multiple things needing to be fulfilled. You will need to have the ability to prioritize what you feel is most important to increase cash flow.

Will doing what you are doing right now, increase or decrease your cash flow? Are you being productive with what you are doing right now? Could this task be achieved when business is at a slower pace? You need to be realistic and instead of working harder, work smarter. Remember, it is not how many hours you put in, but what you do within them hours which count.

CHAPTER

20

TRAINING YOUR
ENTREPRENEURIAL MIND

"I've learned that people will forget what you said, people will forget what you did, but people will never forget how you made them feel." Maya Angelou

Yes, I said your entrepreneurial mind. Oh, you don't think you've got an entrepreneurial mind? False. We all have an entrepreneurial mind; some just never have the need to use it on a daily basis as a requirement to make regular money.

How I would define entrepreneurship?

The first word which comes to my mind personally is survival, my second choice of word would be instinct. I look back on episodes in my life where my entrepreneurial mind was at its peak, I was fully in tune with it's ability, the main factor which contributed to its peak was times of great need.

But because I have a track record of entrepreneurship is this what equals being an entrepreneur? I wouldn't say so, no. Why? Because we all have a track record of being entrepreneurial - I feel there is a difference between being entrepreneurial and being an entrepreneur.

Have you ever sold bits on eBay? Been to a car boot and made a profit? Held a cake stall at school? These are all traits of being entrepreneurial. You probably didn't even notice; you just did it – Why? Because you wanted money, but why didn't you keep it up? Probably because you have a job also, which provides security. When we are in receipt of something regular such as a pay slip we lose the fire in our bellies to seek for more. But hey I guess you can't guarantee eBay or car boots – Or can you?

Mark Radcliffe was 21years old, working for Tesco's when he established his business First2Save on eBay, becoming the first British eBay millionaire. He began using his bedroom to run the business, starting from a £200 investment – It took 10 years to consistently create a turnover of more then £3million per year.

People have made millions out of the craziest most unrealistic ideas. The quote goes-

> *"Being realistic is the most common path to mediocrity." – Will Smith*

I think we can agree on two things so far. Initial outlay in regards to finances is not an excuse. Secondly, thinking something such as eBay or a method you have used in the past to pay your bills as a one off, is not a full time option because it isn't safe, is also not an excuse. What else would I rule out which you may or may not think is hindering your path to success? Failure and a poor background or upbringing. In fact, I think a huge proportion of millionaires became who they are today from at least one, if not all, of the 3 points mentioned.

What would I recommend honestly is the fastest way to becoming an entrepreneur?

This sounds stupid, and I wish I wasn't suggesting it, but to sell everything you have, lose it all, tie weights to everything you own and throw it into the sea. I don't want you to have anything to begin with – This is what truly creates entrepreneurship. OK, there is the rich kid who grew up in a huge manor house, who's dad owns

4 successful companies – Great. What do they lack? The entrepreneur's survival instinct.

When you start with nothing, you have nothing to lose. When you have nothing to lose, you become reckless. When you become reckless, you make urgent and quick risk taking decisions. This enables you to fail fast but learn quicker than others who are not in a similar situation to you are.

I look at people with nothing and do you know what I say? This is great. They look at me like I am crazy. There they are sobbing away and I'm telling them this is the BEST part of their lives! Why? Your survival instinct kicks in, you become desperate, desperation creates innovation. You NEED to feel this, you have to feel this loss and failure and sometimes you need to loose everything to fully understand the message. Besides, how could you possibly teach and add value, if you've always had everything on a plate? What lessons could you possibly teach? Enjoy the struggle, this is the best part – I promise.

Honestly, if we take a look at a couple of the greatest entrepreneurs to have ever lived, where did they come from? Let's see if we can notice a common trait.

- Jan Koum was the co-founder and CEO of WhatsApp before being sold for $19 billion to Facebook in February 2014. Jan Koum immigrated to the U.S from Ukraine 20 years ago and upon arriving had to live on food stamps. He is now worth an estimated $6.8 billion.

- Oprah Winfrey who is said to have amassed a $3 billion fortune to date. Oprah spent much of her childhood living with her grandmother who was so poor she could only afford to clothe her with dresses made out of potato sacks. From living to and throw from her mothers, fathers and abusive homes she decided to turn her life around into the right direction. She was soon noticed by a radio station after winning a beauty pageant – The rest is history.

That's just two examples, there's plenty more. How do we build on what is already there, to use to our advantage in creating eternal freedom? Other than losing everything you have, what else would I suggest makes good qualities for a full time entrepreneur?

- Consistent passion (You need to want this more than you want to breathe)
- Commitment (Entrepreneurship is like your first true love; you would do anything to keep hold of what you have.)
- Being open minded and versatile (Allowing yourself enough slack to enable you to see things from more than one perspective and act accordingly, regardless if you agree or not.)
- The want to learn (Reading books, instead of watching soap operas. Soaking up information which is relevant and concurrent with your end goal)
- Your ability to view yourself in the future (Reverse engineering yourself by viewing where you ultimately see yourself later in time, therefor working backwards from that point to see where to go)
- Infinite numbers of new ideas and improvements. (You should tap into your intuition and act on ideas, regardless how crazy they may seem and work to improve yourself daily)
- Time management and prioritization (Understanding what's important and when it's a priority)
- Avoiding procrastination (Being intentional with the valuable time you have)
- The ability to communicate and listen to others

(Being honest and straightforward with your message, losing your ego and listening to others viewpoints, what you may agree with today, may be different too tomorrow.)
- Confidence (No entrepreneur I have come across shows their self doubting side. We all have doubt, but allowing it to seep through your character is a no when becoming an entrepreneur. "Doubt kills more dreams than failure ever will" Suzy Kassem)
- Determination and persistence. (Giving up is not an option for you)
- The belief of always succeeding, therefor putting yourself in uncomfortable risk taking positions is the normal (Because even if you do fail, to you it isn't failing, it's learning.)

Maybe you are a person reading this book who has already embarked on the journey of entrepreneurship, you already recognize clearly the traits of a successful entrepreneur, since you've put them to practice and understand what works and what doesn't. You could more than likely add to this list.

What about if you are new to becoming an entrepreneur? Or would like to leave your current circumstances to pursue working for yourself? You now understand a few of the traits a successful entrepreneur will show consistently through how they react to their life situations and people around them and their own life.

You have the first part of the equation, knowing you do not want to be employed, but how do you see if you have these qualities?

First of all, a lot of these qualities listed apply to everyday people. Being able to communicate with others with ease, being open minded, having a passion and zest for wanting to improve your life, viewing your life as positive as oppose to negative are all qualities I could name within people who are not entrepreneurs.

But how would you know if you have what it takes to be a full time entrepreneur?

Firstly, throwing yourself into uncomfortable situations. So for example; I never use to enjoy speaking to new people who were in high positions which seemed intimidating. This was due to low self esteem, so how did I conquer this? I began positioning myself in situations where I would have to engage in conversation with people who fit the category which made me feel this way. Soon enough, I began to feel more confident around these people who I would normally feel inadequate around. I began showing my new confidence through my character, my new confidence led to new success, my new success led to new credentials which then made me more valuable and taken more seriously by others.

Whatever is making you uncomfortable, whatever you feel you just could not do. Begin doing.

Write a list of 5 things which intimidate you or make you feel uncomfortable. This could be speaking to corporate suited and booted individuals high up in the food chain like how I once felt myself. Public speaking in front of others, having a shower in the gyms public bathroom naked, speaking to someone you have always wanted to speak too but never had the courage, asking the guy or girl you fancy out on a date, standing up to someone you have always wanted to say something too, joining a gym, joining a networking group but being too self conscious to stand up and explain who you are. These are just examples of things people may fear.

Something which use to always help me get through uncomfortable situations was two things I told myself, regardless if these things were true or not. Number one, I am the greatest of all time, I would whisper this to myself when I felt most vulnerable. Number two, I will never meet these people again, so go for it.

Now you have a clear list of things which make you feel uncomfortable, guess what I'm going to suggest next? Get yourself out there and do it. Because you are the greatest, and this is your life, and it isn't fair on yourself to feel inadequate or intimidated or uncomfortable by anything. Trust me when I say, the new founded confidence you will gain from doing things you hate doing or uncomfortable in doing, will propel you to success and new highs you will never have thought you would experience.

I've never been a confident person, but if you ever met me, you would think I was the most confident person on the planet. I've always been in search for reassurance and approval from others, so it isn't like I'm dishing out the advice but have never felt this way. You need to work on the ability to throw yourself into situations which feel uncomfortable. A true entrepreneur will do things regardless if they feel like doing it or not, this is what separates an entrepreneur from an employee. Even on our bad days, we grind. Because if we waited until we felt good or safe to do something, we would achieve what we achieve in a normal week, in 10 years.

I'll give you a prime example of doing something regardless how you feel within yourself. March 2014, I began a stage in my life where I basically lost the plot. A lot was going on in my life and I began having regular panic attacks and freaking out. This went on for 10 months, gradually getting worse and worse. How I was feeling turned so bad I picked up an eating disorder, anxiety followed by depression.

I couldn't even drink a glass of water that's how bad my

eating disorder was. I lost two stone, had no energy, I couldn't sleep and I couldn't get out of bed in the morning.

Why am I telling you this? - For a boost of inspiration.

Why is this inspiring?

Because I set up my business House Proud Finish in the peak of this nightmare I was living. Although I genuinely could not eat or sleep, although I was regularly experiencing extreme panic attacks, I still set up my cleaning company.

What pushed me through what I went through, which I no longer suffer from?

Sheer determination. Understanding that how I was feeling was temporary, but success was forever. I convinced myself that regardless how bad this was going to get; my future days will be brighter than my days today. I clung on for dear life through these 10 months, and regardless how I felt, no matter how much I thought I could not go on, I did it anyway. You have to believe tomorrow is going to be better.

Another way I pulled myself out of this hole was to educate myself. I began reading and understanding what was happening to me. If I could give any advice to anyone else experiencing anything similar, my advice would be to never categorize yourself. The moment you tell yourself you have something wrong with you, you believe you do. The mind will react to whatever you tell it. If you say, "Hey, I have anxiety" Sure, of course you do, at least you do now. Educate yourself, learn more and become more valuable. Because the more valuable you become, the less likely it is for you to be replaced.

What saved me?

I wasn't being true to myself. I was doing things wrong; I was going against who I was. Understand you are you, and love yourself for that. I'm being serious. You are the person you spend every single minute of every single day with, learn to fall in love with yourself.

What else would I suggest helps tune the entrepreneurial mind?

Networking. It's something I never did myself when I first started out. I come from a rural village in the middle of nowhere, although that's no excuse, there wasn't people around me who were chasing success. People just had jobs, it was all very normal and average. I use to approach people with my opinions and I'd receive the weirdest looks. People around me just didn't get it. Why would anyone want to work 80 hours or more a week for something which isn't guaranteed, you must be crazy? Yeah, I was. I guess I still am, at least in their eyes.

The idea was to do well in school, go to college, then university, get yourself a degree, a well paid job and if your lucky grab a mortgage and have two kids. I guess I ticked off a few of those before I became fed up of mediocrity. Before deciding that it didn't matter who agreed and who didn't with what I wanted. I chose a different path and promised to stay on this path regardless if some weeks I paid myself less than what I would receive in a salary paid job. Old friends began driving round in new cars, initially I was envious, but I thought to myself, do I go down that route and get a new car now but that be it? Or do I stick too what I had planned for me, and buy a new car every week once I made it?

The hurdles are there to breakaway anyone who doesn't really, really want it. Yes, people want it, of course. Everyone wants to be financially free, eternal happiness, to wake up and do as they please. But little do anything to change this, or at least consistently long enough to produce results.

So I now strive to network. I speak to everyone and anyone. I still get many who do not get it, but out of those I approach I find people who do get it. When you finally meet people who truly get it, it becomes such an amazing feeling. You are grateful because you understand these people are rare.

After speaking about being true to yourself, it's also important to understand that not everyone will like you, care about what you are trying to achieve, want to listen to what you have to say or want what's best for you. This is perfectly normal and should never be taken personally. Majority of the time people disagree and want to keep you where you've always been because it suits them and is a reflection of them, not you. You are trying to break free from the mould and they cannot understand why, especially if you've always been the person you've been and suddenly your changing direction.

To become a successful entrepreneur; you need to learn when to say no, not yes. Yes, is easy - no becomes more difficult. This is vital when in the start up phase more than any other phase, because people are going to be coming at you with suggestions, business deals, offers, help, sometimes all disguised as a rip off.

When you find yourself in the start up stage, you understand what you want but you may not have all the knowledge just yet to execute your idea, therefore will be swarmed by third parties trying to take control. It's important to not allow others to take control and change direction of what you initially wanted. I am by no means telling you to not take help from others or not to listen to others suggestions; but learn to say no.

I have found myself in situations where I have lost track of what is going on with my idea because I have given the charge to others. I have been in situations where I have felt intimidated because of my lack of knowledge in a specific field, therefore I have just said yes, when I should have said no, I don't want that thanks. Be assertive in what you want and if you're not sure, ask for more time to reconsider and weigh up the pro's and con's of any suggestions which are being made to you.

Work and home life balance?

If I'm completely honest, I haven't myself figured a fine line balance between the two. It wouldn't be fair for me to lay out a paragraph on what I feel you should and shouldn't do in regards to how much you decide to work, and how much you decide to give to your loved ones. For me it comes down to more of an understanding; I need people to understand my journey and that I am my own human being with my own life. I give a lot of my time to family, especially my little boy, I try to do this also by involving them in my journey.

Before me and my son go out for the day, he will come on the road with me to close some deals, then we take a trip out for the day to do something fun. I've never once tried to pretend this is not me, or that I can be someone who has the time available like an employee. My time is valuable and I have a dream and goals.

From the start I have always made this clear and I guess people eventually understand that this is the life you have chosen. I do personally know plenty of entrepreneurs who decide to shut off at 5pm or 6pm and spend the evening with their families – that's great. For me this is a lifestyle, maybe this view will change as I grow older. There is no right or wrong way, it's whatever suits you and your current circumstances and how understanding people are of your journey.

As an entrepreneur myself, I do feel we are a different species. I know that's a big statement to make, but we are. We are the creators of the mobile phone apps, the inventers of creations which help make life easier, the designers of clothing, websites, platforms to help connect you to your friends, cars which get you to work, the food and drink you consume and more.

Where am I going with this?

I feel as an entrepreneur; you are not recognized until the results are in front of people's eyes. You are not taken seriously until you've produced what you said you would produce. You are given no credit for the journey, only credit for when you reach the destination. Therefor I would like to make this paragraph about giving yourself credit. Stop reading for a second, and just give yourself a pat on the back.

This journey is a tough one to travel - I'm not going to lie; for me the journey has been very emotional. I have lost every friend within my previous circle who I grew up with, my family never took me seriously, even with this book. But what kept me going was a vision. I tell myself everyday, no matter what happens, no matter who supports my vision and who doesn't, it's becoming a reality regardless. It's harsh for me to say, but you come into this world alone, and sure enough you will leave this world on your own also.

I don't want to be bias because amongst us we all have encouraging and supportive people around us, who I myself am very grateful for. But you are important as a person, and you need to give yourself credit and learn to take care of yourself, no one is going to give you the motivation you need, you have to find this yourself.

Execution. Whenever I hear that word I think of a poor

man being executed in the Victorian times – weird I know. This has to be within the top 5 of a true entrepreneur. What separates an entrepreneur from an employee of a company? Execution. Every single person has great ideas. Hey, someone may have even thought of something similar to Facebook before Mark Zuckerberg created it, but what's the difference? Execution.

Mark Zuckerberg created Facebook, not Joe down the road who was thinking about it for 5 years. I honestly am not interested whatsoever in how ridiculous, stupid, unrealistic your idea is. Do it. Do it right now, regardless of what is against you. OK – fair enough, we need to be logical with a risk reward ratio, we have to be careful. Scrap that, I'm kidding. Sorry, careful is no longer part of our vocabulary.

Stop hesitating, reasoning, convincing yourself why it is or it isn't a good idea, and do it. Worry about the consequences later.

Honestly, some people may read this book to obtain a to do list on a business. Although I have included some fantastic ways to market, advertise, obtain funding and research business ideas which I know will serve well to the reader. Nothing will serve better than the uncut, stripped back, raw advice I am giving in my paragraphs about entrepreneurs and mindset. Absorb this information and use it in your everyday life, before you know it, you will be a badass destroying any obstacles in your path, even obstacles 2 miles ahead.

CHAPTER

21

THE END OF THE BEGINNING

"Life has a certain flavor for those who have fought and risked all that the sheltered and protected can never experience." John Stuart Mill

Why have I named this chapter the end of the beginning? Because now you are wise enough to begin your start up, equipped with the tips and tricks needed to successfully launch your own business.

I first want to thank YOU, the reader, for purchasing my book. I have put an extreme amount of effort and time into this piece which I really hope serves you in pursuing your dreams and goals.

For me this has been a huge learning process, and still continues to be so every day which goes by. We cease to learn anymore the day we leave the earth. The aim of the book was never to be a money magnet, the aim was always to try and add value and teach what I have learnt myself.

When I was 7 years old I was diagnosed with Perthes disease, by 8 I couldn't walk and was told by a leading consultant I would never walk again. I spent from the age of 7 until 12 in hospital and 4 of those years on crunches and in wheelchairs. Prior to being diagnosed with Perthes disease I had every friend I could have asked for, I won every sports event yearly and regularly featured in the local newspaper for sports events.

It was a real blow when I found out I'd never walk again and even worse spending 5 years in hospital and loosing out on school life, my friends, sleepovers and everything I should have been doing at 7 years old. I can remember being laid in hospital, unable to wash, go to the toilet, with limited interaction. That time in my life was a difficult time, but throughout that entire experience not once did I ever accept that I would never walk again. They could put me in wheelchairs and crutches, operate on me and put me in hospital beds, but I promised I would walk again. Today I can walk, run and skip.

I guess through this period of my life of silence and loneliness is what created the crave and desire for connecting with others. It's taken me years to realize this and now I want to spend the remainder of my life meeting, greeting and helping others where I can. This is what this book is about, it's an accomplishment for me personally and a gift to you.

If you enjoyed my story and wish to connect with me, visit the Entrepreneurs Platform www.entrepreneurs-platform.com or follow me on Twitter- @BGJBarker Instagram - @EPCREATOR or Facebook – The Entrepreneurs Platform. I would love to hear your story.

ABOUT THE AUTHOR

Benjamin Barker is a young passionate entrepreneur within the UK, owner of two successful companies both established with no outside investment, bootstrapping his way to success. Ben believes entrepreneurs are the new age and generation and his aim is to connect entrepreneurs to one another through a go to platform for business expertise. Ben understands the journey of entrepreneurship, one that at times can be lonely. Ben's mission is to share his knowledge on entrepreneurship and business to help reduce people's learning curve. The aim is to fill the void between the curious and the established. Ben differentiates from other entrepreneurs because his knowledge of business and finance does not finish with figures and methods, but extends further into the actual understanding of people which enables him to reach others from all levels and coach them into achieving their full potential in and out of business.

You can keep up in touch with Ben through his blog:

www.BenjaminGJBarker.co.uk/blog